Designer: Malcolm Smythe
Editor: Catherine Bradley
Art Director: Charles Matheson
Researcher: Cecilia Weston-Baker

Illustrated by
Ron Hayward Associates
and Peter Bull

© Aladdin Books Ltd

Designed and produced by
Aladdin Books Ltd
70 Old Compton Street
London W1V 5PA

*First published in
the United States in 1986 by*
Franklin Watts
387 Park Avenue South
New York NY 10016

ISBN 0 531 10234 3

Library of Congress Catalog
Card Number: 86 50273

Printed in Belgium

CONFLICT IN THE 20th CENTURY

THE FIRST WORLD WAR

Dr JOHN PIMLOTT

FRANKLIN WATTS

New York · London · Toronto · Sydney

INTRODUCTION

In this, the first volume of a series dedicated to a study of conflict in the 20th century, we look at the period 1900–18, with special reference to the First World War. It is a dramatic story and one that needs to be told if the political, social and economic history of the century is to be fully understood. Without it, we would find it difficult to appreciate how the world has developed to its present state. Many of the themes of 20th-century history, such as Great Power rivalry, social change, economic interdependence and total war, have their origins in this early period.

Before 1914, the world was dominated by the European powers. They enjoyed unrivaled political, economic and military strength, but distrusted one another to the extent of creating two armed camps, ready for war. When the heir to the throne of Austria-Hungary was assassinated in late June 1914, this was all that was needed to spark off a cataclysmic conflict that was to last for more than four years.

At first, everyone had expected the war to be short, but developments in defensive weapons, particularly the machine gun, soon produced a stalemate on most fronts. Attempts to break the deadlock by frontal assault led to enormous casualties and to the development of new, more horrific weapons. On the battlefield, massed artillery, gas and the introduction of the tank gave the war a new dimension. In the air, the advent of the bomber brought civilians face to face with the full horror of modern war. At sea, the submarine disrupted trade and threatened whole societies with starvation. By November 1918, about 9 million soldiers, sailors and airmen had lost their lives in the first of the century's "total wars."

Simultaneously, the world changed. Four empires – Imperial Germany, Austria-Hungary, Imperial Russia and Ottoman Turkey – collapsed. Communism enjoyed its first victory. The United States began to emerge as a major power. Britain and France were weakened by their losses and people in all countries grew weary and cynical. The problems of peace were to prove impossible to solve.

DR JOHN PIMLOTT *Series Editor*

EDITORIAL PANEL

Series Editor:
Dr John Pimlott, Senior Lecturer in the Department of War Studies and International Affairs, RMA Sandhurst, UK

Editorial Advisory Panel:
Brigadier General James L Collins Jr, US Army Chief of Military History 1970–82

General Sir John Hackett, former Commander-in-Chief of the British Army of the Rhine and Principal of King's College, London, UK

Ian Hogg, retired Master Gunner of the Artillery, British Army, and editor of *Jane's Infantry Weapons*

John Keegan, Senior Lecturer in the Department of War Studies and International Affairs, RMA Sandhurst, UK

Professor Laurence Martin, Vice-Chancellor of the University of Newcastle-upon-Tyne, UK

British trenches during the Battle of the Somme, July 1916. The first day of the battle produced 57,470 British casualties of whom 20,000 died. They had little battle experience and some had only recently arrived in France. Such appalling losses did not halt the offensive however and it continued until November 13, with British casualties averaging 4,000 a day.

CONTENTS

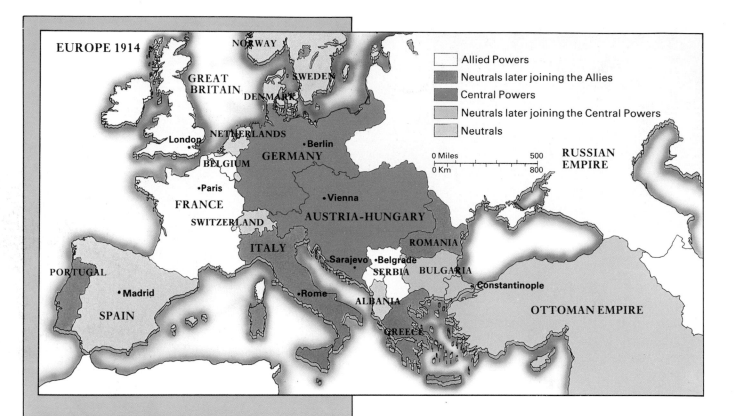

EUROPE 1914

Allied Powers
Neutrals later joining the Allies
Central Powers
Neutrals later joining the Central Powers
Neutrals

CHAPTER 1
THE ROAD TO WAR

Between June 28 and August 4, 1914, the major countries of Europe drifted into war. The assassination of the Archduke Franz Ferdinand, heir to the throne of Austria-Hungary, was blamed on Serbia, a Balkan country under the protection of Russia. As Austria-Hungary demanded retribution and threatened Serbia, Russia mobilized her army, thereby antagonizing Germany, who feared an attack from the east. But Germany dared not move without first destroying the power of France, Russia's ally. As German troops marched westward, France also mobilized her army. Britain followed suit because German advances breached Belgian neutrality. In six weeks, the delicate balance of power in Europe, sustained by an alliance structure which reflected the rivalries and fears of its member states, had been upset. This provoked a cataclysmic four-year conflict that was to change the shape of men's lives forever.

On the morning of June 28, 1914, the Archduke Franz Ferdinand, heir to the throne of Austria-Hungary, and his wife paid an official visit to Sarajevo, capital of the province of Bosnia in the Balkans. During the ride from the railway station, a group of Bosnian patriots threw a bomb. The attack was bungled. When Franz Ferdinand arrived at the city hall, he cut the proceedings short, blaming officials for failing to provide adequate security. As the royal visitors left, the archduke's chauffeur made a wrong turn into a side street. He was ordered to stop and turn around.

As he did so, by an extraordinary coincidence, the car stopped in front of the one remaining conspirator, a Bosnian farmer's son and self-styled "student," Gavrilo Princip. Pulling out his pistol, he ran forward, firing three shots. More by good luck than expert marksmanship, he hit the archduke and his wife and within seconds both lay dead.

Princip was arrested immediately. He was later sentenced to a long term of imprisonment, only to die of tuberculosis a few years later. Within six weeks, this seemingly minor event in a backwater area of Europe had sparked off a major war that was to last for four terrible years.

Left: Franz Ferdinand and his wife arrive at Sarajevo Below: Bosnian police arrest Gavrilo Princip (2nd from right).

Europe in 1914

In order to understand why this happened, it is necessary to look at the political, economic and strategic realities of Europe in 1914. The continent was, in many ways, the center of the world, dominating diplomacy, trade, social development and political ideas. The major powers of Europe – Austria-Hungary, France, Germany, Russia and Great Britain – enjoyed great wealth, exploiting their rising educational standards and new technology to transform raw materials into finished products, although the level of industrialization differed from country to country.

Russia was far less developed than France, Germany or Britain. However in terms of steel production, by 1914 all five of the major powers were great producers. Germany led the way with a staggering 19 million tons a year, followed by Britain with eight million tons, France and Russia with four million each and Austria-Hungary with two million. All these countries also had an elaborate infrastructure of railways to serve their growing industries and markets.

In addition, three of the powers – France, Germany and Britain – had access to cheap raw materials from their empires. Only one other country had the potential to match such wealth, and that was the United States of America, but in 1914 she was still the "sleeping giant" of the world, concerned with domestic rather than world affairs.

However, wealth and power tend to produce rivalry. Before 1914, there was a limit to the markets available for industrial products, leading to friction as each country tried to establish its own monopoly. Clashes also occurred outside Europe as new resource areas were opened up. In places as far apart as Morocco, West Africa, Sudan and Siam (Thailand), crises occurred as the colonial powers clashed at the outer limits of their possessions.

At Fashoda in the Sudan, British and French troops almost caused a European war in 1898 by laying rival claims to the area of the upper Nile. In 1905 and 1911, France and Germany mobilized their naval forces in response to their respective claims to Morocco. In all these cases, diplomatic negotiations prevented war, but their existence indicated how fragile relations were.

The European alliances

Such fragility was reflected even more sharply by changes in the "balance of power" within Europe itself. In the past, the continent had enjoyed some sense of security through the creation of an elaborate yet constantly shifting series of alliances. This worked as long as the center of Europe was occupied by minor German principalities, duchies and bishoprics, which could be played off one against the other to produce a "buffer zone" between the major powers. But the system ceased to function in the 1860s with the emergence of a unified German state.

Under the leadership of Prussia, the idea of a German national identity caught the imagination of people in places such as Brunswick, Hanover and Mecklenburg and helped to establish a new territorial bloc as powerful and wealthy as any of its neighbors. Nor was this a peaceful process: as early as 1866 the Prussians imposed their will by military force on Austria and, four years later, on France.

Such a radical change to the map of Europe had a profound effect upon the alliance structure, helping create a more rigid set of agreements. Both France and Russia feared German expansionism, aware that any move by her, either east or west, could result in war.

Germany also felt insecure, realizing that she was in danger of facing attack from France and Russia, from two different directions simultaneously. Her priority was therefore to ensure that if she were attacked, she would have allies who could threaten the enemy with a similar twin-pronged attack. In the east, Austria-Hungary could threaten Russia, particularly as the two states were already trying to establish control of the unstable Balkans. In the south, Italy could threaten France on Germany's behalf, while in the west Britain could also be approached.

In the years leading up to war in 1914, therefore, Europe settled into two armed camps. In the center were Germany and Austria-Hungary, allied in 1879, and they were joined in 1882 by Italy to form the Triple Alliance, designed to counter French or Russian aggression. Such a solid bloc antagonized the outer powers, and in 1894 republican France and imperial Russia – an unlikely pair of allies, brought together by fear – formed the Dual Alliance.

Britain emerges from isolation

Britain could not ignore the realities of continental Europe, especially when she found her neighbors posing threats to her empire. Relations with France were soured by Fashoda. Kaiser Wilhelm II of Germany was distrusted since his declaration of support for the Boers in the South African War of 1899-1902. Russia seemed intent on policies that threatened northern India. An alliance between Britain and Japan in 1902 diverted Russian attention eastwards – three years later, Russia was heavily defeated by the Japanese on both land and sea – but the only way to counter the other two rivals was to make friends with one against the other.

Germany's declared policy of building a navy specifically to rival that of Britain, together with an enormous growth in German industrial output, made matters worse because it threatened imperial trading links and undermined Britain's traditional markets in Europe. As a result, in 1904 Britain turned to France, forming an *Entente Cordiale* (an informal agreement rather than a rigid alliance). Two years later a series of military "staff talks" began that were to commit British forces to Europe in the event of war with Germany.

Events leading up to war

Such a background of distrust, rivalry and fear helps to make sense of the chain of events which led to war in the six weeks after Sarajevo. The process began predictably enough: as soon as news of the assassination reached Vienna, the shocked Austro-Hungarian government looked for revenge. They blamed Serbia for encouraging the Bosnian nationalists.

In 1912 the people of Serbia, to the southeast of Bosnia, had led a revolt against Turkish rule. For over a year a bitter war had been fought, which resulted in the emergence of Serbia as an independent state. To the Austro-Hungarians, any spread of these nationalist ideas threatened their continued rule of provinces such as Bosnia and Herzegovina.

On July 23, after consultations with the Kaiser, Austria-Hungary presented an unacceptable ultimatum to the Serbs. Serbia was under the protection of Russia, intent on preventing an increase of Austro-Hungarian power in the Balkans, and Tsar Nicholas II responded with a partial mobilization of his army.

This triggered the alliances into action, for as soon as Russia began to mobilize, Germany felt threatened. But if Germany mobilized, she feared an attack in the west from Russia's ally, France.

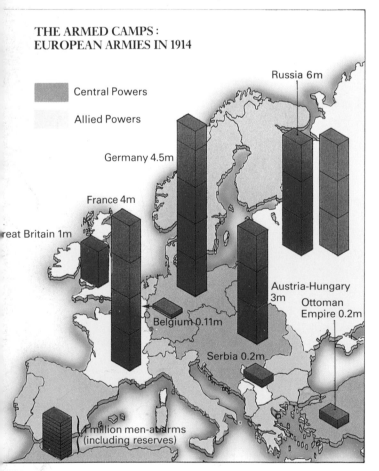

THE ARMED CAMPS: EUROPEAN ARMIES IN 1914

Central Powers

Allied Powers

Russia 6m

Germany 4.5m

France 4m

Great Britain 1m

Austria-Hungary 3m

Ottoman Empire 0.2m

Belgium 0.11m

Serbia 0.2m

1 million men-at-arms (including reserves)

The French wanted to regain the provinces of Alsace-Lorraine lost in 1870. German planners had already catered for this in the so-called Schlieffen Plan, named after a former chief of the general staff, Count Alfred von Schlieffen. According to the plan, German troops would concentrate first against France, knocking her out by means of a massive right-hook through neutral Belgium towards Paris. Then they would move east against the slower-moving Russians. In theory, the plan had much to commend it. After all, the Germans had managed to defeat the French in six weeks in 1870, and that was about the time it would take for the Russians to mobilize. But it did mean that the Kaiser had to take the initiative and declare war on France, even though that country did not yet pose an obvious immediate threat.

That declaration was made on August 3, two days after a similar declaration of war between Germany and Russia. By this time, the first trainloads of German troops were concentrated at Aachen ready to march into Belgium. Once that occurred on August 4, Britain entered the war, accusing Germany of violating an 1839 treaty guaranteeing Belgian neutrality.

Popular feelings

Public reaction to these events varied from country to country. In Russia and parts of Austria-Hungary, where educational standards were low, most people had no idea what was happening and blindly followed their political masters, as they had done for generations. Elsewhere, popular pressure, amounting almost to hysteria, accelerated the slide to war.

In Britain, the popular press whipped up anti-German feeling to the extent that shops owned by people with German-sounding names were attacked and dachshunds were kicked in the streets. In France, the cry was one of revenge for 1870 and the recovery of Alsace-Lorraine. In Germany the fear of encirclement gave voice to demands for immediate military action.

A very small minority – pacifists, trade unionists and socialists – spoke out against the war. But as the armies marched to their destruction, they did so to the cheers of people unaware of the tragedy that was about to unfold. Only the British Foreign Secretary, Sir Edward Grey, seemed to realize that it was the end of an era: "The lamps are going out all over Europe; we shall not see them lit again in our lifetime."

German reservists receive an enthusiastic send-off from Berlin, August 2, 1914. Few would survive the next two months.

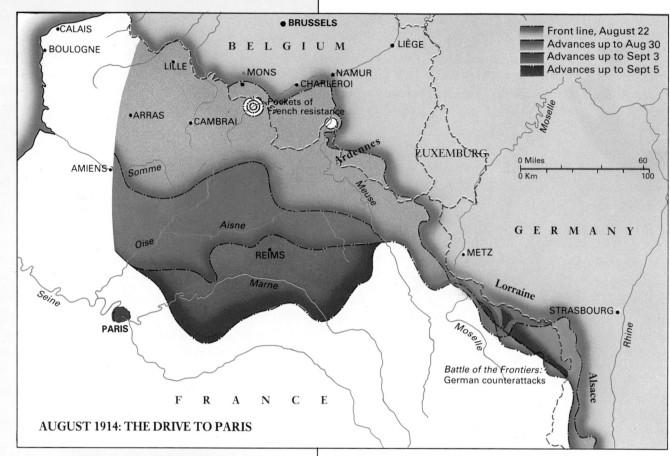

Front line, August 22
Advances up to Aug 30
Advances up to Sept 3
Advances up to Sept 5

CALAIS
BOULOGNE
BRUSSELS
B E L G I U M
LIÈGE
LILLE
MONS
NAMUR
CHARLEROI
Pockets of French resistance
ARRAS
CAMBRAI
Ardennes
LUXEMBURG
Moselle
AMIENS
Somme
0 Miles 60
0 Km 100
G E R M A N Y
Meuse
Aisne
Oise
REIMS
METZ
Marne
Lorraine
Seine
STRASBOURG
PARIS
Moselle
Rhine
Alsace
Battle of the Frontiers:
German counterattacks
F R A N C E

AUGUST 1914: THE DRIVE TO PARIS

CHAPTER 2
THE STRUGGLE FOR EUROPE

The fighting that began in August 1914 was confined principally to Europe. Despite optimistic claims that the war would be "over by Christmas," it quickly degenerated into a costly stalemate. Early maneuver battles failed to achieve decisive results. To escape the effects of artillery and machine-gun fire, soldiers on all fronts dug in, constructing trench lines that were to remain a feature of the next four years of war. On the Eastern Front, the Germans and Austro-Hungarians eventually broke the deadlock against Russian forces weakened by political unrest and revolution. But in the west and in northern Italy, the battles took on a nightmare pattern of heavy casualties for little or no territorial gain. By 1918, the European powers were weary of war and it was only after the arrival of US troops that the Allies could muster the strength to win.

THE OPENING MOVES, 1914

The mobilization plans of France and Germany were notably efficient. In both countries, millions of reservists – men who had completed full-time military training and returned to civilian life, on the understanding that in an emergency they would be recalled to their regiments – reported to their local barracks and were equipped for war. With their comrades in the standing forces, they boarded thousands of trains for the journey to the battle area, after which they would be expected to march towards their chosen objectives. In France alone, between August 2 and 18, 1914, 3,781,000 men were moved in this way, using over 7,000 trains. The timetables were elaborate – at one point, French troop trains were traveling only eight minutes apart – but their very rigidity created a weakness. Once the rival armies had been committed, there was little anyone could do to recall or stop them. At one point when Kaiser Wilhelm had second thoughts, his army commanders informed him there was nothing he could do. Events assumed a momentum of their own.

As far as the French were concerned, the bulk of their forces, four out of five available armies under the overall command of General Joseph Jacques Césaire Joffre, were dedicated to Plan XVII – the recapture of the "lost" provinces of Alsace-Lorraine. The attack began on August 14 with advances on either side of the fortress city of Metz and, at first, all seemed to go well. German border outposts were quickly overwhelmed as French infantry, conspicuous in their red and blue uniforms, sought revenge for the defeat of 1870. But they soon ran out of steam in the stifling summer heat, enabling the Germans, under Crown Prince Rupprecht of Bavaria, to recover from their initial surprise.

On August 20, the Germans counterattacked, catching the French at Morhange and inflicting terrible losses. This set the pattern for the "Battle of the Frontiers" – a French advance followed by a German counterattack – and by the end of the month Plan XVII was in ruins. French casualties were enormous. Over 300,000 men were killed or wounded, including an estimated 10 per cent of the pre-war officer class. It was not an auspicious start.

The German sweep through Belgium

The situation was made worse by the fact that such an emphasis on Alsace-Lorraine diverted French attention and resources away from the main German thrust through Belgium towards Paris. This began as early as August 4, when German troops attacked the border fortress of Liège and imposed the first of a series of crushing defeats on the hastily mobilized Belgian Army. As the latter withdrew through Brussels and towards Namur, the French were forced to take notice, but were hard-pressed to respond.

Joffre had one army in the northeast – under General Charles Lanrezac – and he ordered it to push forward as far as Charleroi. The newly arrived British Expeditionary Force (BEF), on Lanrezac's left, filled the gap between Charleroi and the Channel coast. Once Liège had fallen on August 5, two German armies (a total of 600,000 men) poured into Belgium, sweeping aside all opposition, and were now poised to cross into France and advance on Paris.

By August 22, General von Bülow's army had made contact with Lanrezac and was beginning to push him back. This left General von Kluck's army, on the extreme right of the German line, with an apparently clear passage parallel to the coast. As most of the French reserves had already been committed to an abortive attack in the Ardennes, designed to relieve the pressure on Alsace-Lorraine, there seemed nothing to prevent a decisive German victory.

The Schlieffen Plan did not succeed, for a number of reasons. The German advance through Belgium proved to be something of a nightmare, for although the Belgian Army was swept aside, its resistance at Antwerp and Namur in August tied down German reserves destined for von Kluck and von Bülow.

German infantry soldiers advance across rolling country, vulnerable to artillery and machine-gun fire.

As it was, their armies were faced with long marches through hostile countryside, with little or no prospect of resupply or support. Their lines of supply became stretched. They were running short of food and the men were soon exhausted, slowing down the momentum of advance.

At the same time the threat from Russia in the east materialized far sooner than expected, diverting further reserves, so that when von Kluck suddenly found his way barred by the BEF at Mons on August 23, he was already facing significant problems. The British, despite inferior numbers, managed to inflict enormous casualties – the leading German columns, pressing forward with confidence, were caught in a hail of rifle, machine-gun and artillery fire from concealed positions – and von Kluck was forced to halt.

He resumed his advance the following day, when the British pulled back from positions left isolated by Lanrezac's retreat on their right. However the delay was crucial, enabling Joffre to gather together reserve units and form a new army (under General Maunoury) to the east of Paris.

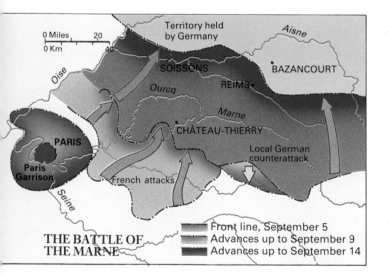

THE BATTLE OF
THE MARNE

Territory held by Germany
Aisne
0 Miles 20
0 Km 40
Oise
SOISSONS
BAZANCOURT
Ourcq
REIMS
Marne
PARIS
CHÂTEAU-THIERRY
Paris Garrison
Local German counterattack
French attacks
Seine

Front line, September 5
Advances up to September 9
Advances up to September 14

The Battle of the Marne

The Germans had made no provision for this sort of redeployment and were caught by surprise when, on September 5, Maunoury mounted a counterattack on the other side of the Marne River. By then, the Schlieffen Plan was in tatters. Von Kluck had followed the retreating BEF and allowed a gap to develop between himself and von Bülow.

More significantly, as soon as Maunoury threatened to fill this gap, von Kluck swung his army around to restore contact with his neighbor, hoping to catch the French in the flank. By doing so, he abandoned the primary aim of his advance, which should have taken him to the west of Paris. Instead, he appeared to the east of the city, allowing the French to concentrate their resources for a major battle, and his lack of coordination with von Bülow left the two armies vulnerable to separate defeat. As the British reentered the battle on September 9 and Maunoury received reinforcements from the Paris garrison, sent to him in taxis, the German advance was finally blocked.

Realizing the danger, the German Commander-in-Chief, General von Moltke, authorized a withdrawal to defensive positions on the Aisne River. As his exhausted troops pulled back, the Allies were slow to follow, needing time to recover from the trauma of recent events. By the time they approached the Aisne, the Germans were already established on the high ground, forcing the British and French soldiers to dig in. A stalemate ensued.

The Race to the Sea

But this could not last, for both armies – Allied as well as German – lacked any support between the Aisne and the Channel coast. It was a tempting gap, offering opportunities for outflanking moves and renewed battles of maneuver, but neither side proved capable of seizing the initiative. As soon as the Germans moved north, so did the Allies, gradually filling the gap with a static front line. By the middle of October the "Race to the Sea" was over, with neither side having gained any appreciable advantage.

In the process, the BEF moved north, to be closer to its supply bases on the Channel coast, and British troops, with the remnants of the Belgian Army on their left, were soon digging in around Ypres on the waterlogged Flanders plain. On October 20 they attempted a final outflanking move towards Bruges, but as simultaneous French advances on their right failed and the Germans counterattacked, they made little progress. By November 11 the hard first battle of Ypres was over, and defensive positions stretched from the Swiss border to the sea.

As the autumn rains gave way to the frosts and snow of a harsh winter, Allied and German troops faced each other from the shelter of trenches, sometimes only yards apart. With the exception of an unofficial "truce" on Christmas Day 1914, when British and German soldiers temporarily forgot their differences and met in the "no man's land" between their lines, the war on the Western Front now entered an increasingly bitter and frustrating period.

Victory on the Eastern Front

This was only part of the story of 1914, however, for battles of equal ferocity were taking place in the east. When the war began, the Germans had only one army – under General von Prittwitz – defending East Prussia. The Germans had assumed that Russian mobilization would take so long that any attacks would be delayed until after the fall of France. In addition, of course, the armies of Austria-Hungary (up to three million strong on full mobilization) could threaten Russian territory in the south. However, as early as August 17, two immense but ill-equipped Russian armies – under Generals Rennenkampf and Samsonov – began a laborious advance into East Prussia, catching von Prittwitz largely unprepared.

Von Prittwitz, defeated on August 19/20 at Gumbinnen, immediately panicked, withdrawing his forces towards Konigsberg, the capital of East Prussia. When he was replaced by the dynamic team of General Paul von Hindenburg and his chief of staff Major General Erich Ludendorff, the Germans soon recovered their nerve. As they did so, a strategic opportunity began to emerge. In East Prussia itself, Rennenkampf and

Samsonov, although superior in str
man forces facing them, were clearly
their actions, for a huge gap, centered
Lakes, gradually opened up.

Seeing an opportunity, von Hindenbu decided to concentrate the bulk of his forces against Samsonov in the south, leaving little more than a thin cavalry screen to face the more cautious Rennenkampf around Gumbinnen. On August 26, at the beginning of a series of actions known collectively as the Battle of Tannenberg, Samsonov was caught in a pincer attack, with German forces converging on his army from both north and south. The Russian army collapsed, leaving von Hindenburg to move against Rennenkampf in the north. The latter did not wait to see what would be the outcome and withdrew.

By September 10, East Prussia had been completely evacuated and, at a cost of over 300,000 men killed and wounded, the Russian offensive had failed. It was an impressive German victory, made possible by the flexibility of interior lines of communication and an inexplicable Russian preference for sending uncoded radio messages.

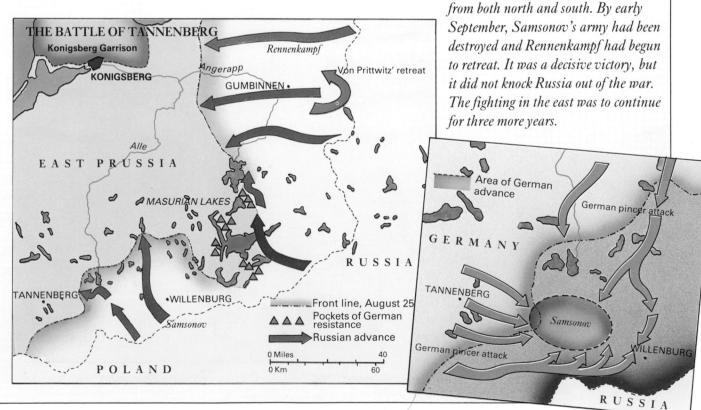

Below: The Russian advance into East Prussia, August 1914, aiming for Konigsberg. As General Rennenkampf advanced from the east, General Samsonov came in from Poland in the south, leaving a gap between the two.

Below: The Germans under General von Hindenburg isolated Samsonov at Tannenberg, converging on his army from both north and south. By early September, Samsonov's army had been destroyed and Rennenkampf had begun to retreat. It was a decisive victory, but it did not knock Russia out of the war. The fighting in the east was to continue for three more years.

THE BATTLE OF TANNENBERG

Konigsberg Garrison

KONIGSBERG

Rennenkampf

Angerapp

Von Prittwitz' retreat

GUMBINNEN

Alle

EAST PRUSSIA

MASURIAN LAKES

TANNENBERG

WILLENBURG

Samsonov

RUSSIA

Front line, August 25
Pockets of German resistance
Russian advance

0 Miles 40
0 Km 60

POLAND

Area of German advance

GERMANY

German pincer attack

TANNENBERG

Samsonov

German pincer attack

WILLENBURG

RUSSIA

Stalemate

Ideally, this victory should have enabled von Hindenburg to switch his forces south, against the right flank of the Russian armies invading Galicia. But the grand design did not materialize, chiefly because the Austro-Hungarians, commanded by General Conrad von Hötzendorf, were finding it difficult to halt the Russian advance. Caught and defeated at Lemberg (August 26-30), von Hötzendorf's right flank was in imminent danger of collapse. He was forced, in early September, to pull back towards Cracow. In desperation, von Hindenburg had to transfer the bulk of his forces from East Prussia to plug the gap, reinforcing von Hötzendorf sufficiently to prevent a Russian breakthrough.

Grand Duke Nicholas, the Tsar's uncle, paused to reform his over-extended formations, concentrating a massive 60 divisions before starting to advance deep into Silesia. The Russian "steamroller" pushed forward, making up for deficiencies in equipment and tactical flair by sheer weight of numbers. Von Hindenburg, now in overall command of the Eastern Front,

saw his chance on November 11, ordering Ludendorff to break into the Russian right flank along the Vistula River. Two Russian armies were defeated around Lodz.

The steamroller had lost what little momentum it had gathered and, as German reinforcements began to arrive from the Western Front in December, Grand Duke Nicholas called off the advance. By the end of the year, the Eastern Front too had degenerated into stalemate, with both sides hastily digging trenches to protect what they already held. On the German side, East Prussia was safe, but for the Austro-Hungarians the campaign had been a disaster, with Russian forces firmly established in Galicia and Warsaw under threat. The simultaneous collapse of an offensive into Serbia merely added to the gloom.

The first five months of the war had therefore been indecisive in all theaters. At an overall cost of nearly a million dead, the major powers had failed to carry out their pre-war plans and, as their huge armies gradually ground to a halt, deadlock followed. Attempts to break that deadlock dominated events for the next four years.

Russian soldiers, captured at the Battle of Lemberg in late August 1914, drag their machine guns into captivity.

A WIDER WAR, 1915

Military strategists found it difficult to respond to the trench system. Soldiers on both sides consolidated their defensive positions, constructing more elaborate dugouts, siting machine guns to cover possible enemy approaches and placing barbed wire in no man's land. Meanwhile, their leaders could not think beyond the idea of frontal assaults to batter through the enemy line by sheer weight of numbers and firepower. Such a strategy was guaranteed to prolong the war, not just because it was doomed to costly failure, but because it meant a revolutionary change in the nature of warfare.

If millions of men and weapons were required, new sources of recruits had to be found and each country's economy put on a war footing, so that it was capable of producing unlimited numbers of guns, shells, rifles, machine guns and bombs. In the process, societies had to change: for the first time in history, all sectors of the population, men and women, had to contribute to the war effort, and the country's wealth had to be devoted to war production. Furthermore, in order to ensure that there was no waste or duplication of effort, governments had to take full control of every aspect of society, deciding what was produced, by whom and for what reason.

The need for such change varied according to the nature of pre-war governments. In some countries, notably Germany, there was a tradition of strong central control, and this was reflected in the relative ease with which they created a war economy. By the spring of 1915, German industry was geared to war and an adequate flow of munitions and manpower had been ensured. But in other countries, where the traditions were more liberal, the problems were acute. This was particularly the case with Britain, which may serve as an example of the social and economic impact of a widening war.

Recruiting the New Armies

When 1915 began, the first priority for all the major powers was to provide fresh soldiers, partly to replace the losses of the previous year but also to prepare for the frontal assaults on the enemy trenches. Among the continental powers – France, Germany, Austria-Hungary and Russia – the pre-war policy of conscription, whereby all able-bodied men were required to undergo a period of military training, had created a reserve of manpower which could still be tapped. In Britain however, the situation was very different.

The British armed forces had always depended on volunteers and, so far as the army was concerned, a significant proportion of these had been killed or wounded in the battles of 1914. A short-term reserve did exist, made up of part-time volunteers (the Territorials), and reinforcements could be expected from the Empire – Australia, Canada, New Zealand, South Africa, India and a host of small colonies – but these were either limited in number or too far away to be of immediate use.

Fortunately, the problem had been foreseen when, at the beginning of the conflict, the Secretary of State for War, Lord Kitchener, called for extra volunteers from the civilian population. Enormous numbers of posters, many featuring the stern face of Kitchener above his pointing finger and the demand "Your Country Needs You," appeared in the streets, persuading men to join up for the "duration" of the war. The aim was to find 100,000 new soldiers, but the response far exceeded all expectations.

The major cities, and even small towns, sponsored the raising of local battalions and young men, inspired by patriotism, a sense of adventure or social pressures (such as when men not in uniform were presented with white feathers as a sign of cowardice), flocked to the recruiting offices. Others came in search of steady employment and some merely followed the crowd, but by the end of 1914 over a million new soldiers were available and that figure doubled within the year.

The military machine was swamped, proving incapable of providing anything, from uniforms and weapons to accommodation and training personnel, for the new recruits. A lack of pre-war industrial organization geared to the needs of the army was partly to blame, but the very process of raising the so-called "New Armies" in 1914-15 also had an effect. Many of the volunteers had occupied key positions in industry, and although there were attempts by the government to prevent certain classes of workers (notably the coal miners) from joining the army, the loss of over two million men from the civilian workforce obviously disrupted the shift to a war economy.

This was felt most severely in 1915, when soldiers fighting on the Western Front suffered a shortage of ammunition, particularly for the artillery. In addition, the New Army battalions had to be clothed and equipped, and in order to cope with this, society had to be transformed.

In spring 1915 David Lloyd George was appointed Minister of Munitions, with the task of ensuring a steady flow of ammunition supplies to the army. New legislation was introduced, designed to increase the power of central government over war production. Women replaced men in a wide range of jobs, including the manufacture of munitions, and the production of non-essential goods was stopped. On a more mundane level, the opening hours of public houses and other drinking establishments were restricted in an effort to reduce worker absenteeism. The war suddenly seemed more serious.

The Spring Offensives

Meanwhile, the battles on the front line continued. In the west, the Germans had decided at the end of the previous year that they could afford to sit behind their defensive lines and let the Allies decide the next move. They also shifted the bulk of their reserves to oppose the Russians, who still occupied positions which threatened the German state. It was up to the British and the French to make the next move. The French could not stand idly by while Belgium and much of northeastern France was under enemy rule.

They had no choice but to mount offensives, ordering their troops to leave the relative safety of their trenches to brave the storm of fire in no man's land. Artillery bombardments might soften up the enemy positions prior to an attack, and it was even possible that a breakthrough might occur. But on the whole the policy of frontal assaults was carried out in desperation by men who soon realized that they were being asked to do too much.

The results were appalling. Between February 16 and March 30, the French lost 300,000 men in Champagne, between Reims and Verdun and in an assault on the St Mihiel salient; between March 10 and 13 the British lost 13,000 at Neuve Chapelle; between May 15 and 27 a coordinated Anglo-French offensive along a line from Festubert to Arras lost 400,000. In each case, the gains were minimal – a few yards of shattered enemy trench, a piece of blood-soaked higher ground, or the remnants of a once-peaceful village. It was as if the Western Front had become an insatiable slaughterhouse, absorbing men as fast as they could be fed into the line.

British women help to manufacture gun barrels at the Coventry Ordnance Works, 1916. It was heavy but essential war work.

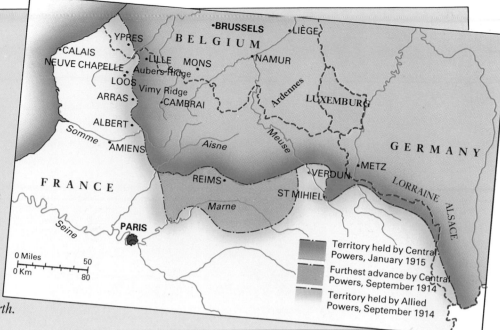

The Battle of Gorlice-Tarnow

It would be wrong to imagine that frontal assaults were always doomed to disaster in 1915. While the Western Front degenerated into mass carnage, German troops in the east, with interior lines of communication and a steady flow of essential supplies, achieved a significant breakthrough against the Russians.

An army, under the command of General August von Mackensen, concentrated a total of 14 divisions and 1,000 guns along a 30-km (18-mile) front between Gorlice and Tarnow to the south of the Vistula River in April. They faced trenches occupied by a Russian army already weakened by poor command and appalling problems of resupply. On May 2, after a four-hour artillery bombardment, special squads of German assault troops (30-40,000 men in all) sprinted forward to seize key enemy positions, only to find that the Russians had already started to pull back. Pouring in his reserves, von Mackensen kept up the pressure, pursuing the enemy as far as the San River, 129 km (80 miles) to the rear. Even this barrier did not stop him: by June 22, Przemysl had been retaken and Lemberg captured, splitting the Russian front in two.

The Russian withdrawal

The time seemed ripe for a decisive blow to knock Russia out of the war. This proved impossible to effect, partly because the Russians were prepared to sacrifice territory to gain time to recover their strength, and also because the Germans depended on Austro-Hungarian reinforcements. Austria-Hungary was now involved in an additional campaign in northern Italy. This occurred because the Italian government decided in May 1915 to join the Allies and sent its forces to attack the Austro-Hungarians in the Isonzo valley on the Adriatic.

The campaign was by no means an Austro-Hungarian disaster – in a series of abortive assaults, the Italians lost over a quarter of a million men before resorting to trench defenses. However, it diverted forces away from the Russian front at a critical time. The Germans had initiated a potentially successful pincer attack against the northern sector of the Russian line in July, when von Mackensen moved north between the Bug and Vistula Rivers to meet with von Hindenburg advancing south from Prussia. But the Austro-Hungarians in the south met with disaster, losing over 200,000 men for little appreciable gain.

The Russians, now under the personal command of the Tsar, fell back to a defensive line which stretched from Riga on the Baltic coast to Czernowitz on the Romanian border, and by late October the front had stabilized. The Russians had been badly hit, losing an estimated two million men in the campaign as a whole and being forced to give up vast tracts of territory.

Just to add to the gloom in the Allied camp, 1915 also saw the Bulgarians join the Central Powers of Germany and Austria-Hungary. They defeated the Serbs. An attempt by the British and French to go to the aid of their ally in the Balkans, by landing an expeditionary force at Salonika, in Greece, failed to affect the outcome. It merely tied down resources that were desperately needed on the Western Front.

In late September the French renewed their offensive in Champagne, with the British mounting a simultaneous assault at Loos, with familiar results. By mid-October over 240,000 men had been lost for minimal territorial gains. The blow was particularly hard for the British, who had now seen the bulk of their Territorials destroyed. Until the New Armies were ready, the BEF could do little but hold the line. Meanwhile, scapegoats had to be found and Sir John French, who had experienced difficulty in coping with the new methods of war, was replaced as Commander-in-Chief of the BEF by General Sir Douglas Haig.

New weapons

Changes in command could not solve the problem of deadlock and other alternatives had to be tried. One suggestion was to bypass the trench system altogether, attacking the enemy where he least expected – a strategy of indirect approach which had failed to achieve a great deal at Gallipoli (see p 35). Another was to develop new weapons which would destroy the advantages of defensive positions.

As early as April 22, 1915, the Germans had come close to a breakthrough near Ypres when, for the first time, they used chlorine gas against the Allies, but that was something of a once only tactical surprise. Thereafter, although gas was to become one of the more horrific aspects of the war, blinding and asphyxiating its victims in large numbers, it was a weapon that could be dealt with by the issue of special respirators (gas-masks) to the front-line troops.

The British were working on another idea. Originally called "landship," but soon given the more familiar name "tank," this was an attempt to produce a mobile armored shell which would be immune to machine-gun fire and capable of climbing over trenches and barbed-wire entanglements to clear a way for follow-up infantry. Its potential was enormous.

All this lay in the future, however, and did not alter the reality of 1915 as a year of mounting losses, enormous social change and a widening of the war as new powers joined in on either side. Without fully realizing the fact, the world was beginning to experience a total war.

Right: A British Mark IV "Female" (machine-gun armed) tank crawls over the lip of a trench during the Battle of Cambrai, November 1917. Inset: A tank crew member in protective helmet and special face shield. His was a hot, noisy and dangerous job.

A HELL-BENT WORLD, 1916

On December 5, 1915, the Allies met for the first time to discuss a common strategy. Gathering at Joffre's headquarters in Chantilly, representatives of the French, British, Russian and Italian armies recognized a basic weakness of the Central Powers – that they were surrounded by enemies and stretched to deal with war on three separate fronts. They agreed to coordinate their campaigns in the coming year. It was a logical decision, designed to deny the Germans and Austro-Hungarians the advantage of switching resources from one front to another as different threats emerged. However it was fraught with practical problems. None of the Allied armies could mount an immediate offensive – all needed to recover from the grievous losses of 1915 – and nothing could be done during the winter weather. The French, still obsessed by the desire to liberate occupied territory, pressed for attacks in early spring, but even they had to accept that the Allies would not be ready much before the summer. Until then, all three fronts would go on to the defensive, with only occasional "spoiling attacks" to keep the enemy guessing.

This would probably have worked if the Central Powers had followed suit and also assumed the defensive, but they had other ideas. Over Christmas 1915, General Erich von Falkenhayn, German Com-mander-in-Chief since the removal of von Moltke a year before, reassessed his strategic priorities. Now that the Russians had been forced back to the Riga-Czernowitz line, the threat to German territory in the east had receded.

Leaving the Austro-Hungarians to tie down Allied forces in northern Italy and Salonika, von Falkenhayn decided to switch the main weight of the German armies to the west, aiming to draw the French (as the more dangerous of the two western allies) into a murderous battle of attrition that would "bleed them white" and leave them begging for peace. Once that occurred, Britain would have to concede defeat.

Von Falkenhayn chose his battleground carefully, believing quite rightly that the French would not respond unless he attacked somewhere crucial to their security or prestige. His eye fell on Verdun on the Meuse River, protected by a string of fortresses and elaborate trench lines. A full-scale frontal assault would be self-defeating, drawing in too many German troops, so he introduced a refinement. Using a massive artillery bombardment (over 1,200 guns), Crown Prince Wilhelm's army would smash the outer defenses of Verdun before sending forward patrols to find and exploit areas of least resistance for the main attacking force. This advance, it was hoped, would force the French to pour in their reserves, which would then be hit by renewed artillery strikes and destroyed. The idea was to inflict maximum casualties for a minimum commitment of German infantry, and to begin with, it seemed to succeed.

Crown Prince Wilhelm (with hands on hips) prepares to distribute medals to his soldiers in the Verdun sector, early 1916.

Verdun

The initial bombardment opened up at 7:15 a.m. on February 21, 1916 along a 13-km (8-mile) front, swamping French forward positions in a deluge of fire which left trenches shattered and the surviving defenders stunned. As the patrols crept over no man's land, they found little resistance and significant gains were made. On February 25, amid snow squalls and a continued artillery attack, the key position of Fort Douaumont was seized by a group of only nine German soldiers, commanded by a sergeant.

This blow to French military pride triggered the very response that von Falkenhayn had planned. General Philippe Pétain took command of the Verdun sector, and the first of what would soon be an endless stream of reinforcements entered the battle area. They found themselves in a living hell: on ground churned up by artillery fire and devoid of vegetation, they occupied shell craters and the remains of a shattered trench system which quickly filled with freezing water. Under constant attack, the French suffered tremendous casualties – one particular unit lost nine-tenths of its soldiers in just one day – but, against all expectations, they held on, gradually sucking the Germans in.

In fact, the seeds of failure for the German plan had been sown before the assault began. The French had recognized the vulnerability of the Verdun sector in 1915 and had begun to improve its defenses, building

An aerial view of the key French fortification at Verdun, Fort Douaumont, before the battle.

new roads and bridges in the rear and strengthening some of the trench lines. The result was a far more effective French response than von Falkenhayn had envisaged. By early March, the *Voie Sacrée* (Sacred Road) leading to Verdun was carrying a daily load of 3,000 trucks, delivering up to 4,400 tons of supplies and 20,000 men.

On March 5 the Germans launched a fresh assault, this time aimed at the northern defenses of Fort Vaux and the aptly named Mort-Homme (Dead Man's) Ridge, but little progress could be made amid bitter hand-to-hand fighting. More and more troops were fed into the battle by both sides.

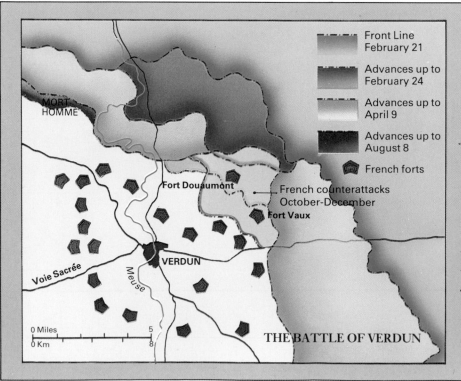

THE BATTLE OF VERDUN

Front Line February 21

Advances up to February 24

Advances up to April 9

Advances up to August 8

French forts

French counterattacks October-December

The Battle of Verdun, February–December 1916

The position of Verdun itself as a bastion on the Meuse River is well illustrated, as are the rings of forts designed to protect it against attack from any direction. The German plan was to break through the forts from the east, flattening them with heavy artillery fire before sending in infantry to occupy the area. It was nearly successful and the key forts of Douaumont and Vaux were captured. However, French counterattacks gradually restored the balance, at enormous cost. Conditions for the soldiers were appalling. The rain and artillery bombardment produced mud which turned to dust in the summer.

Fort Douaumont after the Battle of Verdun: the surrounding ground is a quagmire of shell craters.

On June 9 Fort Vaux fell to determined German attack. But the French were still capable of holding on despite appalling casualties. Indeed, such casualties were by no means one-sided. In early July a single German regiment lost a reported 80 officers and 3,200 men in less than four days' fighting. As the battle raged on, the chances of a German attritional victory slowly faded. The fighting around Verdun continued until December, making it the longest single battle of the war, and by that time nearly one and a half million men (about 700,000 on each side) had been sacrificed for little appreciable territorial gain. The nightmare of war was at its height.

The Battle of the Somme

Nothing could disguise the failure of the Chantilly strategy. On July 1, the long-awaited British contribution to the catalogue of disaster began. The plan was to mount an overwhelming attack against German positions on the Somme River, using five French divisions on the right and the whole of General Sir Henry Rawlinson's army, composed largely of "New Army" battalions, on the left. A huge artillery bombardment, involving over 1,000 guns firing non-stop for eight days, was to be followed by an infantry advance into German lines which, it was confidently predicted, would be little more than heaps of rubble.

Unfortunately, it did not work out like that. The German trenches had been dug deep into chalk ridges along a 40-km (25-mile) front and were not destroyed. Their defenders emerged to man machine-gun posts in time to see the first waves of infantry, weighed down with equipment, plodding towards them across no man's land. In many areas the barbed-wire entanglements had not been cut and the soldiers were funneled into pre-set killing zones.

The result was hideous slaughter. By the end of the day, 57,470 casualties (including nearly 20,000 dead) had been suffered by the British, for no territorial gain. The impact of these losses was tremendous and far-reaching, including heavy casualties among the "Kitchener Battalions," raised in 1914.

French soldiers man a captured German heavy machine gun on Mort-Homme Ridge, Verdun, summer 1916.

Cities, such as Manchester, Birmingham, Liverpool, Sheffield, Leeds, Bradford and others, were forced to recognize the reality of total war. Whole streets as well as entire villages lost their menfolk.

The killing did not stop there, for the offensive could not be called off. At first only localized attacks took place, chiefly to rescue those men who had somehow managed to reach the enemy lines. But by July 14 the British had recovered sufficiently to mount a more concentrated assault. This time the infantry gathered quietly at night in no man's land, without the support of artillery, and against all expectations they succeeded in breaching the German defenses to a depth of nearly 6,000 yards. Their achievement was marred.

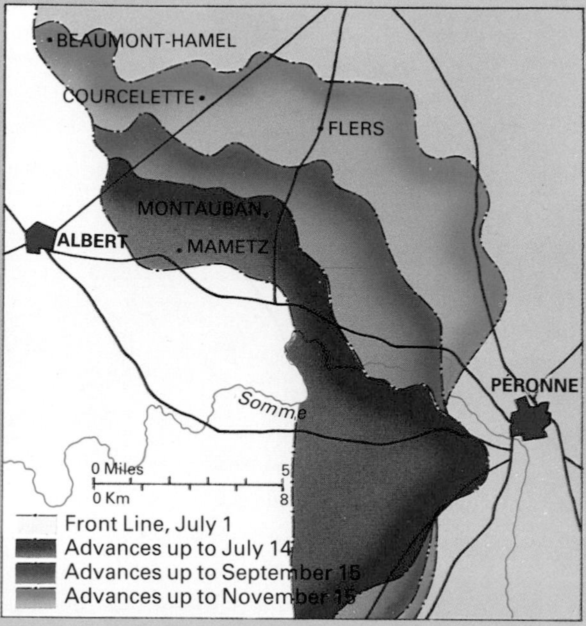

A British 8-inch howitzer battery lays down long-range supporting fire on the Somme, August 1916, but to little effect.

Battle of the Somme, July–November 1916
This shows the painfully slow progress of the British advance. What had been hailed as a major breakthrough, spearheaded by the Kitchener volunteers, quickly degenerated into an attritional battle in which hundreds of thousands of men died.

Map labels: BEAUMONT-HAMEL, COURCELETTE, FLERS, MONTAUBAN, ALBERT, MAMETZ, Somme, PÉRONNE

0 Miles 5
0 Km 8

Front Line, July 1
Advances up to July 14
Advances up to September 15
Advances up to November 15

Without reserves to exploit the gap, the battle continued the familiar pattern of attritional slaughter. Even when, for the first time, tanks were introduced, the results were disappointing, for although the sudden appearance of thirteen of the monsters at Flers-Courcelette on September 15 temporarily produced panic among the enemy troops, the Germans were soon able to recover. All the time, of course, the casualties mounted: by November 13, when the last of the British assaults finally captured the shattered village of Beaumont-Hamel (one of the original objectives on July 1), the British Army had lost a staggering total of 460,000 dead and wounded, a figure that represented twice the pre-war regular force.

The Russian contribution

Similar patterns of useless attrition emerged elsewhere throughout the year. On May 15, for example, the Austro-Hungarians mounted a surprise attack in the Trentino sector of the Italian front, only to be halted and pushed back a month later with heavy casualties. By then the Eastern Front had burst into life again when, on June 4, General Alexei Brusilov advanced without warning against the Austro-Hungarians near the Carpathian Mountains. This was, in fact, the Russian contribution to the Allied strategy decided at Chantilly, and to begin with significant gains were made. But when German reinforcements arrived to plug the gap, Brusilov was forced to a halt.

By September he had lost an estimated million men, with untold numbers deserting to escape the horror. The Russian Army was in a state of collapse, although not before its latest advance had tempted the Romanians to join the Allied cause. This proved to be a disastrous decision, triggering a combined invasion by German, Austro-Hungarian and Bulgarian forces once Brusilov had been stopped. Cut off from Allied aid, Romania fell in December. This provided the Central Powers with much-needed wheat and oil. The only consolation to the Allies was that the campaign, unforeseen at the beginning of the year, tied down even more German resources.

The impact of failure

Therefore 1916 was a year of apparently fruitless sacrifice for all the major powers. The strategies, so carefully worked out at the end of 1915, had failed and the losses in men and equipment had steadily risen to new heights. The effects were far-reaching. On the political scene, governments came under pressure from societies unused to the reality of war.

In Britain, for example, Prime Minister Henry Asquith fell from office in the aftermath of the Somme disaster, to be replaced by David Lloyd George. Those military leaders who had advocated the recent campaigns were dismissed. By the end of the year, both Joffre and von Falkenhayn had been replaced, the former by General Robert Nivelle and the latter by von Hindenburg, and new ideas were being explored in an effort to break the deadly stalemate. More importantly, at least in the long term, societies were being transformed. In Russia the war was increasing the demand for change. In Austria-Hungary the old order was falling apart, and in Germany, France and Britain the casualty lists were hitting at every level of society.

New York American

LUSITANIA DEAD 1,256---115 AMERICANS
GERMANY OFFICIALLY ADMITS SINKING SHIP

U.S. WILL ACT QUICKLY: | HUNDREDS MASSED ON | GERMANY'S OFFICIAL | FROHMAN'S BODY IS
DRASTIC STEPS URGED | DECK AS LINER REARED | STATEMENT | FOUND; VANDERBILT
AS INDIGNATION RISES | IN HER DEATH PLUNGE | | AND HUBBARD LOST

Left: America learns of her losses on the Lusitania, *May 1915. This helped to swing opinion against Germany. The first casualty figures were slightly inaccurate. Some 128 Americans were lost.*

THE DARKEST YEAR, 1917

The winter of 1916-17 in Europe was one of the worst on record. On all fronts, soldiers suffered the additional hardship of rain, frost, wind and snow. The steady drain of casualties did not cease thanks to local attacks, trench raids and artillery strikes. Large-scale military operations proved impossible. It was almost as if nature, appalled at the senseless bloodletting, had imposed its own frozen truce.

This was an ideal opportunity to explore the possibility of peace and, as the winter months progressed, various preliminary moves were made. As early as December 12, 1916, hoping to exploit the effects of the fall of Romania, the Germans offered to negotiate with the Allies. Six days later, President Woodrow Wilson of the still-neutral United States tried to find common ground between the warring powers by requesting definitions of respective war aims. In March 1917 Emperor Karl Franz Josef of Austria-Hungary made an independent approach to France. But the war was too deeply embedded in societies which had already suffered hardship, and the appeals fell on stony ground. By spring of 1917 the military planners had regained the initiative, putting forward schemes for the next round of slaughter.

The United States joins the Allies

President Wilson's interest in the outcome of the war was indicative of a growing concern among Americans. In 1914 they had supported the policy of strict neutrality, and although pressure groups in favor of one side or the other existed, Americans could not overcome a general feeling that the war was of no direct consequence to the United States.

The German advance into neutral Belgium, followed by reports of atrocities against the civilian population,

helped to create a shift in favor of the Allied cause, which was shown by the provision of substantial financial loans. Meanwhile German attempts to impose a naval blockade on the Allied powers disrupted transatlantic trade. American opinion was further alienated by the loss of the *Lusitania*. The blockade intensified on February 1, 1917, when the Germans initiated a policy of unrestricted submarine warfare against all shipping, "that of neutrals included," trading with the Allied powers (see p 41). Wilson responded by breaking off diplomatic relations with Berlin.

A few weeks later he declared war, after the shock of the so-called Zimmermann Telegram had sunk in. This was a diplomatic note, sent by the German Foreign Minister, Arthur Zimmermann, to his representative in Mexico City. It suggested an alliance if the United States continued its recent military operations against Mexico, and a promise to finance a Mexican expedition to "reconquer her lost territory in Texas, New Mexico and Arizona." The effects of the telegram on American public opinion were dramatic. People on the West Coast, in the Midwest and in the southern states, suddenly woke up to the prospect of war on their doorstep and joined the easterners in a clamor for action. On April 6, 1917 Wilson obliged by declaring war on Germany.

It was a turning point in the conflict, promising the Allies a material and human reinforcement that could only be decisive, but which could not be realized immediately. American industry was not geared to war and its armed forces were weak. The Allies could not realistically expect to feel the benefits much before 1918, and even then, would have to supply American units with tanks, artillery and aircraft. Meanwhile the British and French would have to contain and further weaken the Central Powers, maintaining the military pressure throughout 1917, regardless of the sacrifices involved. It was made more difficult by events in Russia, which threatened the Allied advantage of attacking the enemy from more than one direction.

The growing support for war in America:
a poster urges aid to the Allied powers.

The end of tsarist rule in Russia

Pressure for political and social change in Russia had been growing for years, fueled by the corruption and autocratic inefficiency of the tsarist regime. In 1905 Tsar Nicholas had tried to defuse middle-class opposition by setting up a parliamentary assembly known as the Duma. As a weak and ineffectual ruler, he feared its influence and gradually reduced its powers. By 1914 it had no power at all, leaving the conduct of the war in the hands of an imperial bureaucracy which soon proved unable to cope. No attempt was made to create a war economy. Industrial workers and peasants alike were drafted into the army, regardless of the disruption to war production and agriculture.

The campaigns on the Eastern Front were badly managed and, as casualties mounted, central control began to slip. The Tsar and his family did little to help. Nicholas insisted on taking personal command of his army in 1915, isolating himself from the central direction of the war by moving to headquarters far from the capital (St Petersburg). His wife came under the scandalous influence of the "mad monk," Grigori Rasputin. By the beginning of 1917, the army could no longer carry on the war and soldiers were deserting in droves. In early March, food riots in St Petersburg escalated into revolution which quickly spread to other towns and cities. As workers, soldiers and sailors set up local committees (known as *soviets*), the Duma declared a Provisional Government and, on March 15, forced the Tsar to abdicate.

Lenin and the Bolshevik Revolution

The Allies welcomed the change, particularly when the new government reaffirmed its support for the war, but the Germans recognized the potential for knocking Russia out of the war. In April they arranged the passage of a special sealed train from Switzerland to St Petersburg (renamed Petrograd), containing the exiled leaders of the Russian communist party, including Vladimir Ilyich Ulyanov, also known as Lenin. He acted as a catalyst for the workers' revolution, and although it took over six months for him to assert leadership of the *soviets*, his arrival in the capital added significantly to the political chaos.

In July the Provisional Government ordered a new offensive against the Central Powers, but the army could not oblige. A German/Austro-Hungarian counterattack pushed the Russians back. Riga fell and, as Petrograd was threatened, the Provisional Government was overthrown. On November 7 elements of the Communist Party under Lenin's control – the Bolsheviks – seized the Winter Palace in Petrograd and within 24 hours a special "Congress of Soviets" had proposed peace negotiations with the Central Powers. Less than a month later, an armistice was signed at Brest-Litovsk. The fighting on the Eastern Front was over.

Russian soldiers, captured by the Germans in the campaigns of 1916-17. By then, Russian army morale had collapsed.

Canadian troops successfully attack Vimy Ridge, during the events leading up to the Nivelle Offensive in 1917.

This was a major blow to the Allied cause, opening up the prospect of a concentrated enemy assault in Italy and the west, before the main American force could be deployed. It did not help that it came at the end of a year that had seen few Allied successes, for the campaigns of 1917, like those of the previous two years, were characterized by huge casualties for little territorial gain. If the Central Powers could not be defeated while they were also committed to the east, the possibility of Allied survival once the Russians had dropped out seemed remote indeed.

The Nivelle Offensive
The early campaigns of 1917 had been conducted with some optimism, engendered largely by the enthusiasm of General Robert Nivelle, the new French Commander-in-Chief. In a series of inter-Allied conferences during the long winter months, he had persuaded the western politicians to authorize just one more overwhelming "push," this time against a distinctive bulge in the German line in Champagne.

The offensive was to be preceded by diversionary attacks on the Somme, carried out principally by the British, after which the main French assault would smash into the bulge and bring the Germans to decisive battle. Unfortunately, the enemy preempted this by withdrawing from the bulge in late February 1917, occupying prepared defensive positions on the Hindenburg Line several miles to the rear. The move took the Allies completely by surprise.

But the Nivelle Offensive was not abandoned. On April 9 the British mounted their attack around Arras, to the north of the German area of withdrawal, and initially, as the Canadian Corps seized Vimy Ridge, some success was enjoyed. It did not last. Reserve units found it impossible to advance across shell-churned ground, and there were insufficient tanks to make any lasting impact. As the battle degenerated into yet another stalemate, the British and French pinned their hopes on Nivelle.

His offensive began on April 16, but fared no better. Within ten days the Germans had recovered from the initial shock and were inflicting such horrific casualties (a total of 187,000 men) that the attack had to be abandoned. By then the French infantry had endured enough. On May 3 mutinies broke out among units ordered up to the line and these quickly spread. Although the Germans were not aware of it, by the middle of the month the Champagne sector was effectively undefended.

Pétain and the French Mutinies

The French government reacted by dismissing Nivelle and appointing Pétain in his place. It was an inspired choice: the new commander immediately toured the front, visiting all disaffected units, listening to their grievances and promising reform. Selected ringleaders were court-martialed and either shot or deported to the colonies. At remarkably little cost, Pétain managed to restore some sort of order.

Even so, the French were clearly incapable of offensive action and full responsibility for maintaining the pressure on the enemy fell to the British. On June 7, Haig diverted German attention away from Champagne by exploding a number of huge mines beneath their trenches in the Ypres sector at Messines Ridge, followed by a limited offensive to tie down reserves. Some success was enjoyed, but it was not enough to keep the enemy fully occupied. Against his better judgment, Haig was drawn into a sustained and costly battle.

Passchendaele

The Third Battle of Ypres, soon to be known by the more emotive title of Passchendaele, began on July 31. Passchendaele was a small village, designated as one of the targets for the offensive. It was doomed to failure from the start, chiefly because of the weather. Almost ceaseless rain, combined with the effects of artillery fire, turned the ground into a quagmire in which it was not unknown for men to drown.

German defenses were formidable, including specially contructed "pillboxes" which proved impervious to anything less than a direct hit by a large caliber shell. Tanks were useless and, as casualties mounted, the chances of a breakthrough quickly vanished. When the offensive was finally called off on November 12, the British had lost nearly half a million men for little gain. More significantly the survivors, shocked and extremely weary, were close to breaking point. The only consolation was that the Germans had suffered similar losses and misery.

The Hell of Passchendaele

"Dully I hoisted myself out of the mud and gave the signal to advance, which was answered by every man rising and stepping unhesitatingly into the barrage. I . . . followed them calmly into the crashing, spitting hell until we were surrounded by bursting shells and singing fragments, while above us a stream of bullets added their whining to the general pandemonium. . . . Then I saw fellows drop lifeless while others began to stagger and limp; the fragments were getting us and in front was a belt of wire. At this moment I felt my feet sink and though I struggled to get on, I was dragged down to the waist in sticky clay. The others passed on, not noticing my plight until by yelling and firing my revolver into the air I attracted the attention of Sergeant Gunn, who returned and dragged me out. . . .

From . . . all sides came the groans and wails of wounded men; faint, long, sobbing moans of agony, and despairing shrieks. It was too horribly obvious that dozens of men with serious wounds must have crawled for safety into new shell holes, and now the water was rising about them and, powerless to move, they were slowly drowning. . . . We could do nothing to help them. . . ." Edwin Campion Vaughan, Royal Warwickshire Regiment, August 1917.

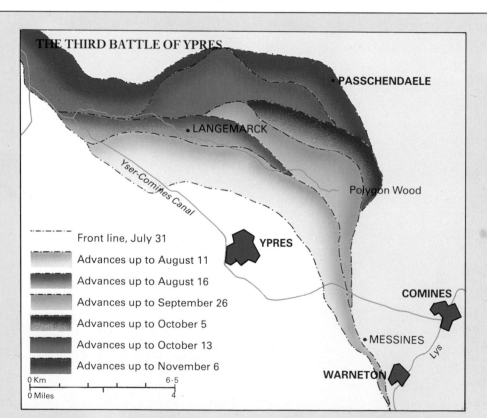

A German "pillbox" at Bullecourt, in the Arras sector.

Equally disturbing news was received from Italy in October, when a sudden Austro-German attack achieved a crushing victory at Caporetto. The Italians avoided complete disaster by withdrawing to the Piave River, but British and French troops had to be rushed to their aid, further weakening the Western Front.

The only relief came on November 20 when a British attack at Cambrai in northern France, preceded by an unusually short artillery bombardment and led by an unprecedented force of nearly 400 tanks, actually broke through the German line. But even this success was short-lived. Lacking reserves to exploit the victory, the British were soon contained and the battle subsided into another stalemate. The offensive capability of massed armor may have been temporarily displayed, but at the time the outcome of Cambrai seemed to be just one more example of the futility of war. As the fourth Christmas of the conflict approached, the Allies faced a growing crisis which only the arrival of the Americans could resolve.

A water cart gets stuck in the mud during the second week of Passchendaele.

THE FINAL CAMPAIGNS, 1918

As the winter weather halted operations in Europe, the two sides struggled to make the most of their respective advantages. For the Germans, the main priorities were to finish negotiations with the Russians and to transfer troops as quickly as possible to the Western Front, before the Americans could make their contribution. For the Allies, the aim was to hold on until the Americans arrived. It was a race that would decide the outcome of the war.

By early 1918, the Germans seemed to have gained the upper hand. On March 3 they signed the Treaty of Brest-Litovsk with the Russians. The new Soviet government agreed to give Poland and the Baltic States (Estonia, Latvia and Lithuania) to Germany and to evacuate Finland and the Ukraine. By then some 40 battle-hardened German divisions had been moved by rail to the Western Front. By comparison, the American build-up was slow – only five divisions had arrived in Europe by February. During the winter the Allies agreed to coordinate military operations through a Supreme War Council, set up at the Rapallo conference of November 1917. This still meant the British and French armies, overburdened and war-weary, were bearing the brunt of defensive responsibilities.

The Somme Offensive

The German High Command, nominally under von Hindenburg, but in reality controlled by Ludendorff, therefore had grounds for some optimism when it came to planning a major offensive, designed to destroy the Allied powers. Ludendorff concentrated a massive force of 62 divisions and over 6,000 guns opposite British positions in the Arras-St Quentin sector, aiming to break through to the coast in an operation codenamed "Michael." The main weight of the attack was to be on the German right, where two armies would advance on Arras, leaving another on the left to set up a barrier along the Somme River to prevent French intervention from the south. In addition, secondary attacks in the Lys and Ypres sectors ("St George I" and "St George II") as well as further south around Reims ("Blücher"), would tie down Allied reserves and create a series of hammer blows which the defenders would be unable to survive or counter.

The Michael Offensive began with a short but incredibly violent artillery bombardment early on

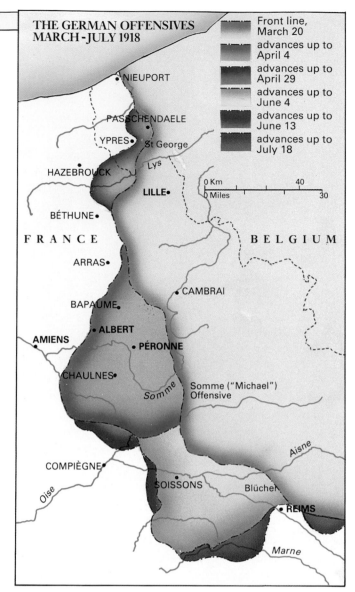

THE GERMAN OFFENSIVES MARCH-JULY 1918

Front line, March 20
advances up to April 4
advances up to April 29
advances up to June 4
advances up to June 13
advances up to July 18

March 21. Before the stunned British defenders could react, special squads of German storm troops emerged from the mist and smoke to attack or bypass key locations. Outnumbered, outmaneuvered and caught completely by surprise, the British fell back along the line, opening a huge gap which Ludendorff immediately tried to exploit.

But the breakthrough did not occur, for while there was little opposition on the left, Ludendorff insisted on concentrating his reserves against Arras, where British defenses gradually hardened. Not until March 28 did he suddenly recognize the potential of the Somme sector, and by then it was too late. Two days earlier, the Allies had agreed to the appointment of the French General Ferdinand Foch to "coordinate" operations on the Western Front (he was formally appointed Allied Commander-in-Chief on April 14), and one of his first acts was to commit part of his meager reserve to plug the Somme gap. By early April, the Michael Offensive had ground to a halt.

Waiting for the Americans

The Germans had managed to advance over 50 km (30 miles), had inflicted over 160,000 casualties on the already-stretched British and had shown just how vulnerable the Allies could be. Realizing this, Ludendorff kept up the pressure and swiftly carried out the second phase of his strategy. On April 9, German troops attacked British positions in the Lys sector, advancing nearly 16 km (10 miles) to threaten the railhead at Hazebrouck before grinding to a halt. On this occasion, despite desperate appeals from Haig, Foch refused to commit his dwindling reserve, forcing the British to rush reinforcements from England and to order the withdrawal of divisions from other theaters.

Foch's decision was justified on May 27 when 22 German divisions attacked the French along a line between Soissons and Reims, sweeping across the Aisne River and reaching the Marne, close to Paris. It was a stunning blow, weakened only by the German inability to cross the Marne. Instead, as the assault divisions gradually lost momentum along the north bank of the river, Foch rushed his last reserves forward to set up a defense which included, ominously for the Germans, a machine-gun battalion of a newly arrived US division, deployed to Château-Thierry.

On June 1, the Supreme War Council agreed to coordinate all Allied shipping and concentrate it on the task of transporting US troops across the Atlantic. By the end of the month, over a quarter of a million troops under General John "Black Jack" Pershing had arrived in Europe. Although they were in many cases unprepared for the nightmare of war on the Western Front, they brought with them a confidence and freshness that revitalized the Allied war effort.

Pershing was under strict orders from Washington to retain his forces as an independent command, avoiding any use of them merely as reinforcements to British and French units, but despite the controversy thus caused, the results were decisive. The Germans, weary from four years of combat, could not match this influx.

The Doughboys arrive: British soldiers rest by a French roadside as an American infantry unit marches confidently past.

This did not mean that the fighting was over. By early June, Ludendorff had created three "bulges" or salients in the Allied line – two large ones near Arras and Reims and one smaller one along the River Lys – and it was imperative that he should try to "straighten the line" by capturing the ground in between. He concentrated initially on the "tongue" of Allied territory to the east of Compiègne, attacking both flanks on June 9. The offensive was poorly coordinated, however, enabling the French, ably supported by US forces at Belleau Wood and Vaux, to hold on. By the end of the month the Germans had lost the initiative.

The Black Day

The Allied counteroffensive opened on July 18 when, in what became known as the Second Battle of the Marne, Foch launched attacks from both flanks of the Soissons-Reims salient. Commanded in the field by Pétain, French and US forces swept forward, spearheaded by more than 300 light tanks which quickly broke through the hastily prepared German defenses. As it happened, most of the German troops escaped before the pincers snapped shut, but for the first time Ludendorff was forced to transfer units from elsewhere to hold the line.

Foch seized his chance, ordering Haig, Pétain and Pershing to mount a series of attacks all along the Western Front, aiming to maintain the pressure and prevent a German recovery. The main blow fell on August 8, when General Sir Henry Rawlinson's army, supported by a French army on the right, struck east from Amiens into the Arras salient. Led by 456 tanks, Australian and Canadian troops broke through in the center. They advanced eight miles on what Ludendorff called "the black day of the German army in the history of the war." Despite hardening resistance on August 9, the Allies were beginning to build up momentum.

Foch made sure they did not lose it. Over the next few weeks (August 10-September 29), he ordered attacks all along the line: in the north around Lys, in the center towards Bapaume in the Amiens sector and in the south towards Soissons and Reims. As an unexpected bonus, the Americans made their contribution even further south when, on September 12, they caught German forces by surprise in the St Mihiel pocket, taking 15,000 prisoners and 450 guns in less than 36 hours. Two weeks later, the whole of Pershing's army and a French army advanced into difficult country between the Meuse River and the Argonne forest in the southern sector of the Soissons-

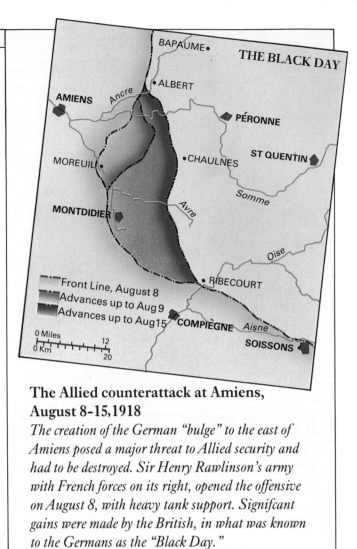

THE BLACK DAY

Front Line, August 8
Advances up to Aug 9
Advances up to Aug 15

0 Miles 12
0 Km 20

The Allied counterattack at Amiens, August 8-15, 1918

The creation of the German "bulge" to the east of Amiens posed a major threat to Allied security and had to be destroyed. Sir Henry Rawlinson's army with French forces on its right, opened the offensive on August 8, with heavy tank support. Significant gains were made by the British, in what was known to the Germans as the "Black Day."

Reims salient. Although they found the going hard – with a breakdown of communications and problems of resupply – the pressure was being maintained.

German problems became acute on September 29 when Haig attacked the formidable defenses of the Hindenburg Line by conducting a huge pincer move against Maubeuge in the south and Ghent in the north. Enemy resistance crumbled, and although the fighting was by no means easy, substantial territorial gains were made. The fact that German reinforcements, rushed north to plug the gap, were jeered by their compatriots and accused of being "war-prolongers," indicated how low morale was. Ludendorff's men could still inflict enormous casualties – in October alone, the British lost a staggering 5,438 officers and 115,608 soldiers – but their resolve was draining away.

The collapse of the Central Powers

Germany's allies were also under attack. As early as September 15, Allied forces had mounted a sudden attack. An offensive was launched in Salonika and within two weeks Bulgaria had been forced to negotiate

The war is over: American troops celebrate news of the armistice on the Western Front, November 11, 1918.

for peace. A month later, after crushing defeats in the Middle East, Turkey capitulated (see p 37), to be followed by Austria-Hungary. Indeed, the latter had been under pressure since June, when yet another offensive in northern Italy had been contained on the Piave River, and in late October the Italians counter-attacked. On October 30 they won a resounding victory at Vittorio Veneto, splitting the Austro-Hungarian armies in two. On November 4 an armistice was finally signed.

The effects of these surrenders were clearly signifi-cant, producing a growing sense of isolation among the German people, but it was events in Germany itself that precipitated the end. Food shortages and industrial unrest had been increasing throughout 1918, and when this was combined with an increase in revolutionary activity, inspired by the Russian Revolution, the very fabric of society began to disintegrate. Uprisings in Kiel, Lübeck, Hamburg and Munich threatened the authority of the central government. The Grand Fleet refused to put to sea, in what its sailors regarded as a pointless suicide mission against the Royal Navy. The desertion rate in the army increased dramatically.

A new government, led by the moderate Prince Max of Baden, tried to prevent complete chaos by appealing to President Wilson, whose "Fourteen Points" of January 8, 1918 had created a framework for peace, but he was in no mood to listen. In desperation, Prince Max persuaded the Kaiser to abdicate on November 9 and sent negotiators to talk to the Allies.

The conditions were harsh – the Allies insisted on an immediate evacuation of all occupied territory, includ-ing Alsace-Lorraine, a demilitarization of the Rhine-land, the surrender of substantial war stocks and weapons, an annulment of the Treaty of Brest-Litovsk and the release of all Allied prisoners of war. With growing evidence of military collapse on the Western Front and the threat of anarchy at home, there was very little alternative.

At 5 a.m. on November 11 an armistice was signed in a special railway carriage at Compiègne. Six hours later – at the eleventh hour of the eleventh day of the eleventh month – the fighting stopped. The quiet was uncanny.

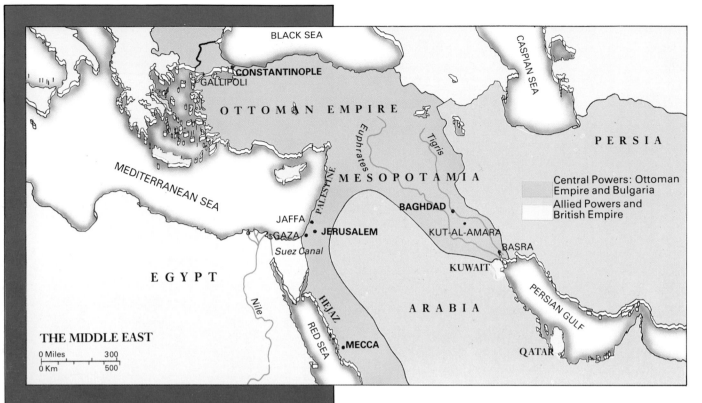

THE MIDDLE EAST

0 Miles   300
0 Km   500

Central Powers: Ottoman Empire and Bulgaria

Allied Powers and British Empire

CHAPTER 3
ALTERNATIVES TO ATTRITION

The fighting in Europe dominates any history of the First World War, but it would be wrong to imagine that this was the only area affected. For while the armies battled it out in the trenches of France and Flanders, the mountains of northern Italy or the plains of Galicia, other campaigns – across the empires of the major powers, in the oceans of the world, and in the air above their armies and homelands – were being conducted with equal determination. In all cases, the aim was to provide a "magic solution" to the problem of European stalemate – to find some way to defeat the enemy without the need for endless sacrifice. Although none succeeded, all contributed to the global, far-reaching phenomenon known as "total war."

SIDESHOWS

One of the advantages of enjoying free passage of the oceans in wartime is that it allows a state to choose alternatives to direct confrontation with its enemies. If costly battles are being fought in one area, troops can be carried by sea to mount attacks elsewhere, approaching the enemy from an unexpected or comparatively undefended direction. This can force the enemy either to accept defeat or to divert valuable resources away from the main conflict to deal with the new threat. This is known as a strategy of "indirect approach" and was favored by the British in wars against more powerful European rivals. When the stalemate in Europe became apparent in late 1914, therefore, it was a strategy that seemed to offer an opportunity to weaken the Central Powers.

At first, the aim was to seize German colonies, cutting off the supplies of raw material and food so essential to long-term survival. By the end of October 1914, New Zealand units had seized Samoa, Australian forces had marched into New Guinea and captured German radio stations throughout the South Pacific, Japanese troops had taken the fortress of Tsingtao on the Chinese coast and the African colony of Togoland had been invaded.

Operations elsewhere took time to organize – The Cameroons and German South West Africa were not cleared until early 1916 – but to all intents and purposes, the German overseas empire had ceased to exist before the war was three months old. Only in East Africa did the enemy put up a fight, when General von Lettow-Vorbeck, commanding a force of less than 5,000 men, conducted a brilliant guerrilla campaign. This eventually absorbed the attention of 130,000 Belgian, British and South African troops in 1917, but few supplies reached Germany from this area once the fighting began.

Turkey joins the Central Powers

When Turkey joined the Central Powers in late October 1914, new opportunities for the indirect approach arose. Although ruled by the dynamic Young Turk party under Enver Pasha since 1909, Turkey was undeniably weak, maintaining a tenuous hold over territorial possessions – the remnants of the once-powerful Ottoman Empire – in the Balkans and the Middle East.

But her army, trained and commanded by German officers under General Liman von Sanders, could not be lightly dismissed and her strategic position on supply routes between Russia and the Western Allies could not be ignored. Thus, when elements of the Turkish Army attacked Russian positions in the Caucasus in October 1914, Grand Duke Nicholas swiftly called for Anglo-French operations elsewhere to relieve the pressure and guarantee the supply route into the Black Sea.

Presented with such demands, the British and French turned their attention to the strategically vital straits, connecting the eastern Mediterranean to the Black Sea through the northwestern part of Turkey. If these could be seized and the Turkish capital of Constantinople (Istanbul) on the Bosporus attacked, Enver Pasha would be forced to abandon his campaigns elsewhere and might be so hard-pressed that he would negotiate for peace.

Gallipoli

Initially, the Allies favored a purely naval operation, sending a powerful fleet of battleships to bombard Turkish forts at the western end of the Straits (the Dardanelles) in February 1915. Some success was achieved, but when the Turks responded by releasing a floating barrage of mines which caused substantial damage, the fleet was hurriedly withdrawn. If the

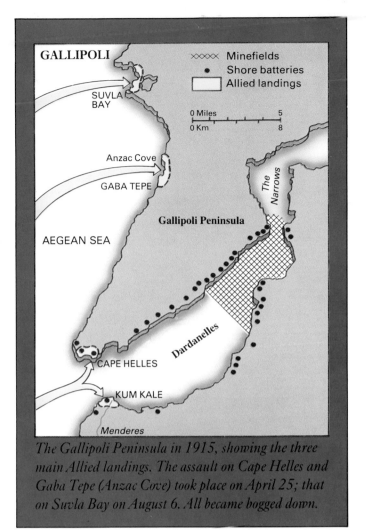

The Gallipoli Peninsula in 1915, showing the three main Allied landings. The assault on Cape Helles and Gaba Tepe (Anzac Cove) took place on April 25; that on Suvla Bay on August 6. All became bogged down.

Dardanelles were to be cleared, ground forces would be needed to seize the forts and occupy the two banks – the Gallipoli Peninsula on the left and the Turkish Asiatic coast on the right.

Unfortunately, because of commitments to the Western Front in Europe, troops were not easy to find. The decision to mount an expedition under General Sir Ian Hamilton was taken in late March, but it took time to gather the necessary forces. In the end, British regulars were detached from the garrison of India and the newly formed Australian and New Zealand Army Corps (ANZAC) was made available, together with the Royal Naval Division (made up of naval reservists acting as infantry). These troops, untried in battle but raring to go, bore the brunt of the early fighting.

On April 25, 1915, the British waded ashore at Cape Helles, at the southern tip of the Gallipoli Peninsula. ANZAC units landed north of Gaba Tepe (soon to be nicknamed Anzac Cove) on the west coast to cut across the center of the peninsula, and French troops attacked Kum Kale on the Asiatic bank.

The River Clyde *under fire, Cape Helles, April 25, 1915.*

Their reception was devastating as Turkish units, personally commanded by von Sanders and heavily reinforced since the naval attacks of February–March, poured down artillery and machine-gun fire from concealed positions on the high ground.

The British were among the worst hit, especially on "V" Beach in the Cape Helles sector, where the steamer *River Clyde*, hastily converted into a landing ship, was caught in the full force of enemy fire. As men walked ashore on specially constructed catwalks, they were swept away by machine guns, dropping into shallow waters that were soon running bright red with blood. Australian casualties at Anzac Cove were also heavy and Hamilton even contemplated ordering their withdrawal. It was not an impressive start.

Establishing a bridgehead

But the Allies held on, carving out narrow footholds on the rocky, scrub-covered shore and, in a depressingly familiar pattern, digging trenches to protect themselves from enemy attack. As losses mounted and disease

Australian troops charge forward, Anzac Cove, August 1915.

began to decimate the ranks, a stalemate developed, forcing the Allies to send reinforcements they could not afford. By July, Hamilton's command had been increased to 12 divisions (almost half a million men) and on August 6 he renewed his assault, ordering the forces at Anzac Cove to break out to the east, while a fresh landing went in to their north at Suvla Bay.

The aim was to cut across the peninsula, isolating the Turks from their supply bases, and at first this met with some success. But it was short-lived. As ANZAC troops gradually lost momentum among the rock-strewn gullies of Gaba Tepe and the British units at Suvla Bay failed to exploit their initial advantage, the attritional stalemate was resumed. Hamilton was relieved of his command and his replacement, Sir Charles Monro, had no hesitation in recommending an evacuation of the peninsula.

The British government, worried about the rising casualty rate, reluctantly agreed. By December 20, Suvla Bay and Anzac Cove were abandoned, to be followed by Cape Helles on January 9, 1916, all without serious incident. But the cost of the campaign had been high – the Allies lost a total of 265,000 men, with many more rendered useless through disease. The experience of war in the unforgiving climate and terrain of Gallipoli had a profound effect on all who took part. The indirect approach was clearly proving to be an expensive business.

Mesopotamia

This was made equally apparent when the Turks were attacked much further south, in Mesopotamia (Iraq), by British-Indian forces sent to secure the vital oilfields of the region. At first the commitment was small – in November 1914 a single division seized the port of Basra at the tip of the Persian (Arabian) Gulf – but when the Turks responded by mounting a counter-attack in early 1915, reinforcements had to be deployed to face the threat.

In April, British forces under General Nixon took the offensive, advancing in two columns towards Kut-al-Amara, on the road to Baghdad. The right-hand column, commanded by General Townshend, enjoyed remarkable success, defeating the Turks near Kut and pushing forward as far as Aziziyah.

Supply problems forced a halt and Townshend withdrew to the apparent safety of the Kut fortress, only to find himself besieged. As food and water ran out and disease swept through the garrison, the British were forced to surrender on April 29, 1916.

Victory in 1917

But Mesopotamia was not abandoned. A new commander, Sir Stanley Maude, spent the rest of 1916 reorganizing the forces at Basra, prior to another drive on Baghdad in December. A surprise attack along the Tigris River forced the Turks into a hasty retreat. Although they rallied sufficiently to prevent complete disaster, they could not stop Maude from entering Baghdad on March 11, 1917.

It was the only bright spot in an otherwise disastrous year for the Allies, but once again the cost had been high. By 1917, Mesopotamia was absorbing nearly half a million troops, whose appearance on the Western Front in Europe might have tilted the balance. Far from the indirect approach dispersing the enemy, it seemed in grave danger of preventing an Allied concentration of force where it mattered most.

Palestine

Even so, the pressure on the Turks was maintained, for while Maude was clearing Mesopotamia, other British forces were attacking the province of Palestine in the eastern Mediterranean. Operations in this region had begun as early as October 1914, when Turkish troops had tried to advance towards the Suez Canal across the Sinai Peninsula (part of the British protectorate of Egypt), but they had failed to make much headway.

The unofficial surrender ceremony at Jerusalem, December 1917.

Thereafter, the two sides settled into an uneasy stalemate, concentrating their attention on gaining the support of local tribesmen. In this the British were surprisingly successful, making the most of a revolt against Turkish rule by Hussein ibn Ali, the Sherif of Mecca and the King of the Hejaz (Arabian Peninsula).

This diverted Turkish attention sufficiently to allow a British advance designed to regain complete control of Sinai. The villages of El Arish and Rafah, on the borders of Palestine, were taken in late 1916 and early 1917, but attacks against Gaza a few months later were repulsed. By then nearly a quarter of a million British troops had been committed to the theater.

Turkish defeat

The failure at Gaza had unforeseen results, however, for in its aftermath the British appointed a new commander, General Sir Edmund Allenby, who wasted no time in revitalizing his troops. At the same time, the Sherif of Mecca was given additional support, including the services of a hitherto-unknown British officer, T E Lawrence ("Lawrence of Arabia"), who helped to organize an Arab revolt in the Hejaz. As the Turks withdrew forces from Palestine to cope with this threat to their rear, Allenby went on the offensive.

By mid-November 1917, he had captured the port of Jaffa, well inside Palestine, and on December 9 he marched in triumph into the religiously symbolic city of Jerusalem. Further advances were delayed by the need to divert troops to the Western Front to counter the Somme Offensive, but when Allenby renewed operations in September 1918, the Turks had clearly had enough. With Lawrence's tribesmen pushing up from the south and Allenby's forces closing on the River Jordan, Turkey negotiated for peace on October 30.

The value of the indirect approach

In the light of these developments, it might be argued that the indirect approach had worked in the end, but that does not disguise the fact that it had been a costly method of waging war. The campaigns in Gallipoli, Mesopotamia and Palestine had tied down significant numbers of British troops at a time when the Western Front in Europe was desperate for reinforcement. Politically, the "sideshow" campaigns may have been worthwhile – victory in Mesopotamia and Palestine put Britain in a strong position after the war to assert control of key areas of the Middle East – but militarily, they were of doubtful value. Once again, the alternative to attrition had not been found.

THE WAR AT SEA

When the war began in 1914, each of the major powers possessed a navy, designed to carry out the twin tasks of protecting coastal waters and maintaining maritime trading routes. Neither Russia nor Austria-Hungary depended heavily on foreign trade – both states could, theoretically, feed their people and equip their armies from internal resources. France could survive so long as the relatively short sea route to North Africa was kept open, but the same could not be said for either Britain or Germany. They needed access to their colonies as sources of raw materials and food, and although Germany could sustain her economy longer from indigenous or neutral European sources, both countries faced the prospect of starvation if denied free passage of the world's oceans. Indeed, in the case of Britain, it was estimated that the country would run out of food in three months if outside supplies were cut off.

A navy's task in such circumstances was clear – to protect maritime trading routes while disrupting those of the enemy. Both Britain and Germany had prepared for such a strategy before the war began, building large fleets of "big-gun" battleships, protected by battle cruisers, destroyers and submarines. These would dominate ocean areas and prevent the movement of supplies by threatening to blow any enemy ships out of the water.

Of the two fleets, that of the Royal Navy was the stronger in 1914, containing a total of 29 battleships based on the revolutionary "Dreadnought" class of ironclads, first launched in 1906. But the British had to cover an immense area, ranging from the coastal waters of the Channel and North Sea across the Atlantic, Indian and Pacific Oceans, all of which required a naval presence to keep trade routes open.

By comparison, the German High Seas Fleet, although smaller in size (18 battleships in 1914), could concentrate on preventing a blockade of domestic ports. It could use the protected harbors at Cuxhaven, Wilhelmshaven and Kiel as bases for raids into the North Sea to keep the British at bay and allow merchant ships to enter German waters in safety. At the same time, individual warships or independent squadrons could go out into the oceans of the world to attack British trade from the colonies. If Britain was to survive, these advantages had to be reversed.

The destruction of the German raiders

The fact that this was achieved in the first few months of the war was a major victory for the Royal Navy, and it was carried out at remarkably little cost. As early as July 29, 1914, the Grand Fleet sailed north under the command of Admiral Sir John Jellicoe, to take up its war stations at the Scottish ports of Rosyth and Scapa Flow. Its appearance in this area effectively deterred the Germans from seeking a major fleet action. As the German High Seas Fleet remained firmly in harbor, other elements of the Royal Navy escorted the BEF to France without interference, made offensive sweeps into the North Sea and gradually cleared the oceans of enemy warships.

Some of the latter did cause damage. Between August and November 1914, the light cruiser *Emden* created panic in the Indian Ocean before being caught and sunk. On November 1 the armored cruisers *Scharnhorst* and *Gneisenau*, under the command of Vice-Admiral Maximilian von Spee, destroyed two British armored cruisers off the coast of Chile.

But in early December a large British force closed in on von Spee, catching him in waters to the southeast of the Falkland Islands in the South Atlantic and destroying his squadron. Elsewhere, individual German warships were overwhelmed – the last to go was the light cruiser *Dresden*, sunk off the coast of Chile in March 1915 – and British naval supremacy was secure.

Meanwhile, the Royal Navy also dominated the North Sea, where the Germans had tried to assert their strength by sending warships to bombard the east coast of England. At first they enjoyed some success – on November 2, 1914 the Norfolk coast came under attack and a month later Scarborough, Whitby and Hartlepool were all shelled – but this did not last. When a third such raid was mounted on January 24, 1915, British battle cruisers under Admiral Sir David Beatty were waiting and, in an action off the Dogger Bank, the German force was destroyed. The German High Seas Fleet withdrew to the protection of its bases, and surface actions in waters so obviously controlled by the Royal Navy were temporarily suspended.

A British "Bellerophon" class battleship lays down supporting fire from her main armament, Suvla Bay, August 1915.

The U-boat Campaign

The Germans could not afford to follow a purely defensive naval strategy and searched for ways to impose a more effective blockade on British ports. On February 4, 1915, in a dramatic change of policy, the Kaiser proclaimed the waters around the British Isles to be a "war zone," through which all ships, neutral as well as British, traveled at their peril, and sent *Unterseebooten* or U-boats (submarines) to implement his declaration. At the same time, enormous numbers of mines were laid along likely sea routes close to the British coast.

Taken together, these policies of indiscriminate action completely changed the nature of the naval war, extending it to affect the shipping (and livelihood) of neutral countries. Of the latter, the US was by far the most important, gradually shifting its sympathies towards the Allies as US citizens were killed. As early as March 28, an American life was lost when the British liner *Falaba* was torpedoed, but far more significant was the sinking of the Cunard liner *Lusitania* on May 7. Out of the 1,198 casualties, 128 were Americans.

President Wilson could not stand by and allow such incidents to pass unchallenged. As they continued, he increased the diplomatic pressure on Germany, even threatening to declare war in April 1916 if the sinkings did not cease. When this was combined with lack of impact on British trade (in 1915 Britain was losing an average of 79,695 tons of merchant shipping a month – mainly to U-boats but also to mines), the Kaiser had no choice but to abandon the U-boat campaign.

The Battle of Jutland

This failure probably helped to spur the Germans to seek a major fleet action, hoping to break the deadlock in the North Sea by destroying the strength of the Royal Navy. The commander of the High Seas Fleet, Vice-Admiral Scheer, initially tried to lure Beatty's battle cruisers out of Rosyth into a submarine ambush, but met with little success. Then, on May 31, 1916, he sent his own battle cruisers under Vice-Admiral von Hipper to make a show of raiding merchant shipping along the Norwegian coast, and this did the trick. As Jellicoe reinforced Beatty with four fast battleships and sent him to investigate, Scheer put to sea with his main force of 16 dreadnoughts and six older battleships.

The two battle cruiser forces clashed late on May 31 and, in a short engagement, Beatty came off worse, losing the battleships *Queen Mary* and *Indefatigable*. By

now, however, Jellicoe had also put to sea and, as Scheer tried to trap the remnants of Beatty's force, the latter hastily disengaged and pulled back towards the Grand Fleet, sailing down from the north. This drew Scheer towards Jellicoe's battle line, and in a series of clashes known as the Battle of Jutland, the rival fleets faced each other for the only time during the entire war.

Their meeting was not decisive. Although the British lost more ships than the Germans (three battle cruisers, three cruisers and eight destroyers to one old battleship, one battle cruiser, four cruisers and five destroyers) they were able to recover far more quickly. However, the effects were far-reaching. The Germans spent the remainder of the war with their surface fleet effectively bottled up in the North Sea ports.

Renewed U-boat Offensive

Once again, the U-boats seemed to be the only possible means of imposing a blockade. Despite their recent failure, a new campaign was initiated, taking advantage of the fact that the High Seas Fleet no longer needed submarine protection. At first, the undersea attacks were restricted to the Mediterranean, where few American ships operated, and some success was achieved (one U-boat managed to sink 72,600 tons of merchant shipping in a single five-week cruise). Moreover, British and French countermeasures, already familiar to the Germans, proved ineffective. They ranged from the simple expedient of hoisting false colors, to deploying armed "Q-ships" disguised as

U-boat sinkings

When the First World War began, no one was aware of the potential of submarines for disrupting an enemy's maritime trade. Since the Germans were prevented from using their High Seas Fleet, they turned to their U-boats as a means of attacking Britain, and soon discovered the advantages. In 1915, U-boats were sinking 69,663 tons of British shipping a month. In 1917, the Germans adopted an "unrestricted" campaign, and total losses rose dramatically. Some 3.7 million tons was lost in that year alone. In 1918 the total fell to a more manageable 1.9 million tons.

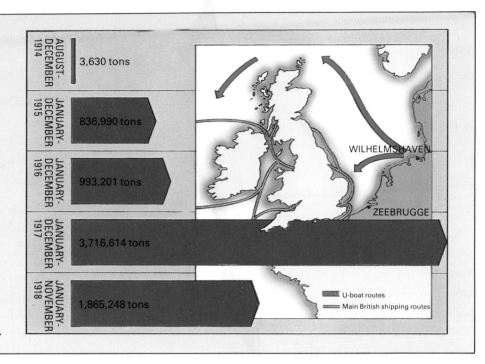

AUGUST-DECEMBER 1914	3,630 tons
JANUARY-DECEMBER 1915	836,990 tons
JANUARY-DECEMBER 1916	993,201 tons
JANUARY-DECEMBER 1917	3,716,614 tons
JANUARY-NOVEMBER 1918	1,865,248 tons

WILHELMSHAVEN
ZEEBRUGGE

U-boat routes
Main British shipping routes

merchantmen. As the campaign was gradually extended back into the North Sea and Atlantic, the Allies began to feel the effects.

In January 1917, the British lost a staggering 411,400 tons to the U-boats, and this tempted the Germans to go one stage further. On February 1, they began an "unrestricted" submarine campaign, in which all ships suspected of trading with the Allies would be attacked without warning anywhere in the world. President Wilson responded by severing diplomatic links with Germany – the declaration of war followed two months later – and the war at sea entered its crucial phase.

Containing the U-boats

The battle revolved around the ability of Britain to resist the steady strangulation of her trading routes, particularly those across the North Atlantic. In the early stages, she came perilously close to defeat. During the first three months of 1917, she lost a total of 470 merchant ships. In April, one ship in every four which left British ports failed to return. As food stocks dwindled and neutral ships were reluctant to carry British goods, urgent measures were needed.

The most effective of these was undoubtedly the organization of convoys of merchant ships, traveling together under naval escort. Despite initial opposition from the Admiralty, obvious success on the run from Gibraltar to Britain in May meant that the convoy system was adopted on the transatlantic routes. By then

the US Navy was also available – indeed, its appearance in European waters under Admiral William Sims was arguably the most crucial effect of America's entry into the war – and shipping losses fell dramatically.

The campaign came to a head in May 1918, when 14 submarines (out of a total of 125) were destroyed, and thereafter the threat rapidly subsided. By the end of the war in November, the U-boats had been driven from the North Atlantic and prevented from returning by the laying of an enormous mine barrage across the 290-km (180-mile) passage between Norway and the Orkneys. While this was going on, submarine bases close to Britain had been raided, most spectacularly on April 22, 1918, when British forces destroyed the harbor at Zeebrugge, and the High Seas Fleet was kept firmly contained in its home ports. The Allied navies enjoyed complete freedom of the seas.

One effect of this was to impose on Germany the very blockade that she had attempted against Britain and, as food became scarce, civilian morale dropped. When Britain had felt the pinch in 1917, she had responded by extending the system of rationing to cover most foodstuffs, but this was nothing compared to the situation in Germany a year later. By then the government had been forced to restrict the flow of all commodities from potatoes to clothing.

As the great influenza epidemic swept through Europe in 1918, the German people fell victim in droves, increasing the pressure to make peace. For that, the Allies had their navies to thank.

THE WAR IN THE AIR

One other possibility existed in the search for an alternative to European land deadlock, and that was to use air space, avoiding the trenches by flying over them to attack targets in the enemy rear. This was not immediately apparent, chiefly because the aircraft was such a new weapon of war. The first manned flight had been carried out by Orville and Wilbur Wright in Kitty Hawk, North Carolina as recently as December 1903, and although the major powers all had aircraft at their disposal in 1914, no one was really sure how best to use them on the battlefield.

At first, aircraft were used for observation and reconnaissance, with pilots reporting what was happening on "the other side of the hill." Some success was achieved, especially by Allied airmen on the Western Front during the maneuver battles of 1914, but the advantage did not last. Ground troops discovered that slow, canvas-covered biplanes were vulnerable to machine-gun fire and both sides quickly developed special "scout" or fighter aircraft to "blind" the enemy by destroying his reconnaissance machines.

The latter had to be protected by their own fighters, so that by 1916-17, entire squadrons or "circuses" of interceptors, led by "aces" such as the British Albert Ball and the German Manfred von Richthofen (the "Red Baron"), were battling it out for air supremacy over the trench lines. Nor was this their only role, for as soon as one side gained free passage over enemy positions, the same aircraft could be used to drop small bombs onto supply dumps, artillery parks or troop concentrations. By 1918, the now-familiar airpower tasks of tactical bombing, ground support, fighter interception and reconnaissance had all been firmly established as routine.

Strategic bombing

But none of this could break the trench deadlock. It was not until the idea of bombing had been extended beyond the battle area to the destruction of targets in the enemy homeland, where factories and their workers produced the weapons of modern war, that the possibility of strategic success emerged. The aim was relatively simple: instead of sending an aircraft to hit an artillery piece on the front line, it could be sent to bomb

Zeppelin L53 is prepared for its first raid on England.

the factory that produced the artillery piece.

The Germans were the first to carry out "strategic bombing" raids, sending huge Zeppelin airships across the North Sea at night to attack targets in eastern England, but the effects were limited. Despite an understandable degree of civilian panic as the silent airships dropped their bombs indiscriminately over the English countryside in 1915, a combination of poor weather, accidents and fighter interception led to mounting German losses and, in mid-1916, the campaign was cancelled.

The German bombing campaign

The emphasis then shifted to the use of special long-range aircraft and, after experiments against Russia in 1916, when *Riesen* or R-type bombers (appropriately known as "Giants") attacked targets more than 480 km (300 miles) beyond the front line, permission was granted for daylight operations against London to begin. On May 25, 1917, 21 twin-engined Gotha GIV biplane bombers flew over the Channel from bases in occupied Belgium, and although they failed to reach London because of dense cloud, they did drop over five tons of bombs onto Folkestone in Kent, killing 95 people and injuring a further 260.

Eleven days later, the pattern was repeated over Sheerness, and when London itself was finally attacked on June 13, the results were significant. In a raid lasting 20 minutes, 14 Gothas flew majestically above the capital in broad daylight, dropping 72 bombs which caused widespread damage. Altogether, 162 people were killed, including 18 children sheltering in a school in Poplar, and 432 were injured. On July 7, a similar attack killed 57 people and injured 193, suggesting that the Germans had discovered a new and potentially devastating method of warfare.

Signs of civilian panic emerged. On July 7, for example, a mob of up to 5,000 angry, frightened people ran riot in the East End, barricading the streets and smashing shops displaying German names. For some time afterwards, civilians showed a marked reluctance to report for work, particularly in the vital munitions factories of the capital. Reports that only one of the Gothas had been shot down in the two raids merely reinforced the fear that London was now wide open to attack and, with public pressure increasing, the government was forced to act. As fighter squadrons were hurriedly redeployed to protect southern England, a special committee, chaired by the South African General Jan Smuts, was set up to investigate the problem.

Smuts' recommendations

The Smuts Committee made two reports, both of which were compiled in haste. The first, presented to the Cabinet in early August, outlined an elaborate London Air Defense Area (LADA), comprising belts of fighter stations, early-warning systems and anti-aircraft guns. This was put into effect without delay. It took time to perfect – a series of night-time Gotha raids in late September/early October, known as the "Raids of the Harvest Moon," continued to inflict damage on London and cause civilian panic – but by the end of the year, the balance was tilting in the defenders' favor.

By December, the Germans experienced losses of up to a third of their force and when winter weather closed in, the campaign faltered. It was resumed in the spring of 1918, but by then the British people had learned to live with the bombing and LADA was fully operational. On May 19 the last Gotha raid on London took place, in which six of the bombers were shot down by fighters and an amazing barrage of 30,000 anti-aircraft shells. An effective air-defense system seemed to have evolved.

Setting up the Royal Air Force

This was not a memory of the campaign that persisted. Smuts in his second report, submitted on August 17, 1917, recommended a counteroffensive. As this would require special aircraft dedicated to strategic bombing, Smuts had suggested the creation of an independent air force free from the demands of the battlefield. Although the idea was initially rejected, the Harvest Moon raids soon altered the government response. On April 1, 1918 the Royal Air Force was formed and preparations began for a series of bombing raids on Berlin and the Ruhr.

In any case, the war ended before an RAF bombing campaign against Germany could begin in earnest. But with the widely held belief that the bomber would always get through to spread panic and destruction in civilian areas, the groundwork had been laid for the massive aerial devastation of World War II. The trench deadlock of 1914-18 may not have been broken by the bombing, but there was now a general acceptance that ordinary people were legitimate targets of total war. It was a frightening development.

Buildings destroyed by a Zeppelin bombing attack in Maldon, Essex, 1915. Indiscriminate raids affected civilian morale.

GREAT BRITAIN

NORWAY

SWEDEN

DENMARK

NETHERLANDS

BELGIUM

GERMANY

FRANCE

SWITZERLAND

ITALY

PORTUGAL

SPAIN

ESTONIA

LATVIA

LITHUANIA

EAST PRUSSIA

POLAND

CZECHOSLOVAKIA

AUSTRIA HUNGARY

ROMANIA

YUGOSLAVIA

BULGARIA

ALBANIA

GREECE

SOVIET RUSSIA

TURKEY

	Western Powers
	Germany and Turkey
	New States

0 Miles 500
0 Km 800

EUROPE AFTER THE PEACE SETTLEMENTS

CHAPTER 4
THE IMPACT OF WAR

The First World War had traumatic and far-reaching effects. In purely human terms, the suffering was enormous, and not just among the millions of fighting troops. The civilian populations also suffered, especially in areas subject to economic blockade, aerial bombardment or enemy occupation. At the same time, societies were permanently affected by the pressures of war. They were forced to mobilize all available resources and to impose unprecedented central control to ensure a coordinated war effort. In the process, new social and political forces were released, ranging from the revolutionary violence of Russia, to the less dramatic, but equally significant, pressures for civil rights among trade unionists, women and ethnic minorities elsewhere. The peace treaties changed the face of Europe by creating new countries in central Europe. By 1918, the "old order" had disappeared in a welter of blood, leaving the exhausted, war-weary survivors to create a safer, more balanced world from the chaos. It was a daunting task.

The failure to find any alternative to the costly attrition of war in Europe – in outlying areas, at sea or in the air – condemned the major powers and their allies to a match of unprecedented violence. What had begun as an essentially limited conflict, became a total war in which all resources were exploited in pursuit of complete victory. In the process, entire societies became involved and the full weight of industrial capacity and technological invention was used to produce even more destructive weapons of war. By 1918 the world had changed. The social, economic and political forces unleashed by the First World War had helped to destroy the old order, leaving a vacuum in which uncertainty, fear and violence could spread.

In purely human terms, the cost of the war was appalling. Between August 1914 and November 1918, about 9 million soldiers, sailors and airmen were killed, often in circumstances of unmitigated horror. Up to 20 million suffered serious injury and an unknown number – probably as many again – suffered long-term psychological damage. The memory of war was etched deep in the minds of an entire generation. There were also an estimated five million widows and nine million orphans, their families torn apart by machine guns, gas and high explosive.

By 1918 over 10 million people in Europe were homeless refugees, caught up in war or revolution, while others had experienced the impact of aerial bombing or suffered the effects of starvation brought about by the naval blockade. Many were so weakened, in fact, that they could offer little resistance to the global epidemic of influenza which reached its height in the closing months of the war, leaving more than 20 million dead in its wake. The effects were significant: in France, for example, 1.3 million soldiers and civilians had been killed, casting a shadow over the survivors. The numbing effect of ceaseless death took a long time to wear off.

The social effect

There was more to the war than that, for in order to create armed forces capable of inflicting and sustaining such losses, whole societies had to be mobilized and existing patterns of life abandoned. As the war progressed, by far the most pressing demand was for soldiers, forcing countries to introduce or extend conscription, regardless of its effects upon society. Mainland European countries already had large conscript armies when the war began, but even they had to cast the net wide, recalling reservists and accelerating the training of each new crop of 18 year olds as soon as they became available.

Elsewhere, as in Britain in 1916 and the United States a year later, conscription had to be introduced for the first time, leading to fears of government control and the suspension of individual liberty. At the same time, the removal of such large numbers of fit young men from the economic sphere, inevitably produced strains at the precise moment when agricultural and industrial efforts needed to be increased. In France, for example, agricultural yields fell by between 30 and 50 per cent during the war years. In Germany the production of wheat was reduced by nearly 60 per cent in the same period. A similar shortfall in colonial supplies because of the naval blockade and, in the case of France at least, the loss of significant industrial capacity in areas occupied by the enemy, merely made the situation worse.

What each state needed was a centralized, closely controlled war economy, geared specifically to the production of weapons and other military supplies, and it was this above all that changed society. At first, the problem was submerged beneath the wave of nationalist fervor that greeted the war, but as mobilization and armed-force expansion drained manpower away from agriculture and industry, governments were forced to act. In some cases, it was almost too late. In France, 52 per cent of all industrial establishments had closed down in 1914 as their workers were recalled for military service, while in Britain, the flood of volunteers to join Kitchener's New Armies left many key sectors of the economy desperately short of trained men.

The war economy

In response, the French government had to withdraw 300,000 skilled tradesmen from the armed forces in 1915 – in Britain the figure for the same year was 40,000 – and relocate them in war work. By then the need for weapons, especially artillery shells, was acute, and an enormous expansion of the munitions industry was undertaken.

The impact of war on ordinary people: Polish refugees flee from the battle area with what they can salvage.

Between 1915 and 1918, the munitions workforce in France increased from 50,000 to 1,780,000 people; in Italy by 1918 over 60 per cent of the entire industrial working population was making weapons.

A substantial proportion of these workers had, by necessity, to be drawn from sectors of the population not normally employed to do heavy or skilled work. By 1918, for example, Britain was employing 800,000 more women in industry than had been the case four years earlier. In the United States a similar development affected the black population, many of whom moved from the rural south to the industrial north as soon as opportunities arose.

In neither case was the trend a permanent one. At the end of the war, returning soldiers reasserted their right to such work, while the economic slump and depression forced many women back into domestic work. But the fact that traditionally oppressed elements of society had shown themselves perfectly capable of contributing to the war effort, undoubtedly boosted their demands for civil rights in the future.

The growth of trade union power

One of the results of growth of the war economy was a significant increase in the size and influence of trade unions. In the United States, union membership rose from two million to 3.25 million in 1917-18; in France from two to three million between 1914 and 1918 and in Britain from four to eight million over a similar period. In most cases, union leaders cooperated closely with management, but militancy increased as they began to realize their power. Even when the war was at its height, there were strikes in key industrial sectors. In 1917, for example, engineering workers in Britain stopped work, as did copper miners in the United States.

By 1918, real wages in Britain had risen by 20 per cent against pre-war levels, and most workers were employed on a basic 48-hour week. Standards of living rose, and so did costs, helping to fuel an inflationary spiral that caused major crises in the post-war period. By then, political parties of the left had received a substantial boost and they gave voice to working-class demands. These were triggered off by the experience of war and the realization that the old social order was not only unjust, but also unable to deal with a national emergency. Indeed in Russia, where the communists exploited the social disruption caused by wartime industrial expansion, the old order was swept away in the chaos of revolution.

The changing role of women: a London bus conductress, 1918.

Propaganda

Faced with such pressures and aware of the desperate need to create social mobilization to fight the war, governments invariably resorted to propaganda, painting the enemy as evil and the war as a crusade, in an effort to retain public support. As soon as hostilities broke out, posters appeared on every street, exhorting people to join the armed forces, register for war work or contribute to special loans introduced to help pay for the conflict. Some of the appeals were blatantly patriotic – "Your Country Needs You" – while others were unashamedly emotional, with pictures of wives and mothers sending young men off to battle – "The Women of Britain Say Go!"

The results were initially encouraging, particularly when reinforced by similar campaigns in the press or newly popular cinema. In later months, hatred of the enemy was sustained through specific campaigns which exaggerated reports of atrocities. British stories of German soldiers butchering women and babies in Belgium had a profound effect in the United States.

At the same time, much was made of military "victories," with newsreels and photographs of brave soldiers, many of whom had never been near the front line. But as the war dragged on and the impact of casualties was felt in every town and village, much of this backfired, creating a cynicism that was difficult to dispel, even after the fighting was over.

Increased government control

This left governments with little choice but to impose control, forcing their people to accept the sacrifices for final victory. An example of this in Germany was the severe "Law of Siege," introduced in 1914. Similarly in Britain the Defense of the Realm Act (DORA) allowed the government to put forward a wide range of new regulations, including restrictions on the opening hours of public houses. At the same time, the British government introduced "summer time," whereby all clocks were advanced an hour to create longer periods of light in the evenings for agricultural work.

Systems of rationing were also introduced, controlling the flow of food according to government priorities. In most cases these were coordinated by new central agencies – the Ministry of Food in Britain, the Fuel and Food Administration in the United States and the splendidly named Imperial Potato Office in Germany. As with so many other aspects of the First World War, these measures did not survive the war (with the exception of public house licencing hours and summer time in Britain), but patterns had been set that were to be repeated in future conflicts.

If the crisis of 1914-18 did nothing else, it familiarized societies with the demands of total war and gave them experience of the centralized control and social sacrifices needed to sustain a modern war effort. As a reaction to such hardships, moral standards in most societies declined as people sought what pleasure they could in the middle of the nightmare.

But these developments, affecting ordinary people and the way they lived, pale into insignificance beside the wider impact of the war on the international scene. In economic terms, the four years of fighting fueled inflation and disrupted traditional trading patterns to such an extent that a return to "normality" was impossible, not least because of the sudden growth of the United States as a manufacturing and commercial center. It was up to the victorious powers – Britain, France, Italy and the United States – to forge a new international order out of the chaos.

The peace treaties

The result was an ambitious package of peace treaties, hammered out at Versailles in 1919 and imposed on the defeated Central Powers. The overall aim was to prevent a repetition of the slide to war in 1914, principally by so weakening Germany, Austria-Hungary and Turkey, that they would be incapable of causing trouble in the future.

In territorial terms, Germany lost her colonies and Turkey her possessions in the Middle East. Austria and Hungary were made into separate, smaller countries, losing territory to help form new countries in central Europe and the Balkans. The latter – Poland, Czechoslovakia and Yugoslavia – were designed to satisfy pre-war pressures for national self-determination, which was seen as a key factor in the causes of war in 1914. However there was also the added advantage of containing the Central Powers within a series of buffer zones.

The process was taken one stage further in the west, where France reoccupied Alsace-Lorraine and insisted on a demilitarization of the Rhineland. Germany was further weakened by being allowed armed forces of no more than 100,000 men, armed with "defensive" weapons only. She also had to agree to the payment of huge reparations to victorious powers as compensation for war damage.

Finally, this "new order" was to be monitored and controlled through a special League of Nations, capable of discussing and settling minor disputes. In theory, the world should have been a safer place. In reality, the problems were only just beginning.

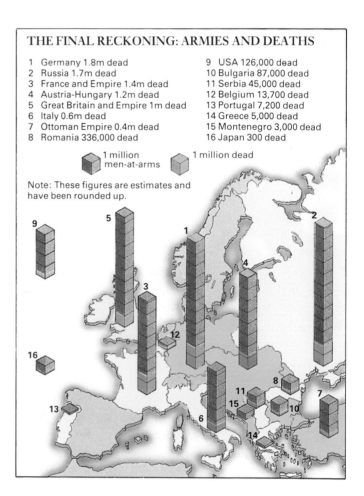

THE FINAL RECKONING: ARMIES AND DEATHS

1 Germany 1.8m dead
2 Russia 1.7m dead
3 France and Empire 1.4m dead
4 Austria-Hungary 1.2m dead
5 Great Britain and Empire 1m dead
6 Italy 0.6m dead
7 Ottoman Empire 0.4m dead
8 Romania 336,000 dead
9 USA 126,000 dead
10 Bulgaria 87,000 dead
11 Serbia 45,000 dead
12 Belgium 13,700 dead
13 Portugal 7,200 dead
14 Greece 5,000 dead
15 Montenegro 3,000 dead
16 Japan 300 dead

1 million men-at-arms   1 million dead

Note: These figures are estimates and have been rounded up.

CONFLICT IN THE 20th CENTURY: APPENDICES

Between 1914 and 1918, the major countries of the world fought a bitter conflict, exploiting all the latest technology and ideas in the pursuit of victory. Leadership, in both political and military terms, was of crucial importance, bringing to the fore personalities who, by the nature of their jobs, seemed larger than life. These appendices are designed to provide additional information. They look at selected leaders and important tactical developments on land, at sea and in the air.

PERSONALITIES

General Alexei Alexeyevich Brusilov (1856-1926), regarded as the most impressive Russian general of the First World War. In 1914, he helped to win a notable victory against the Austro-Hungarians at Lemberg, and in 1916 he commanded Russian forces in a major offensive which came close to success. Appointed Commander-in-Chief under the revolutionary government in 1917, he went on to join the Red Army in the Civil War.

Georges Benjamin Clemenceau (1841-1929), French Premier and Minister of War, 1917-20. A radical politician, nicknamed "The Tiger," he was responsible for hardening French resolve at a critical time in the war and, thereafter, for imposing harsh terms on the defeated Central Powers.

Marshal Ferdinand Foch (1851-1929), Allied Commander-in-Chief in 1918. A soldier dedicated to "the offensive," he proved flexible enough to cope with the trench deadlock, replacing Nivelle as French Commander-in-Chief in 1917 and accepting the difficult role of co-ordinating Allied operations during the crisis of early 1918. He made a significant contribution to eventual victory.

Field Marshal Sir Douglas Haig (1861-1928), Commander-in-Chief of British forces on the Western Front, 1915-18. A cavalry officer of courage

Marshal Ferdinand Foch

and experience, he commanded I Corps of the BEF in 1914 before taking over First Army a year later. In late 1915 Haig assumed command of British forces, bearing responsibility for the major battles on the Somme (1916), at Passchendaele (1917) and during the traumatic days of 1918.

Field Marshal Paul von Hindenburg (1847-1934), Commander-in-Chief of the German Army, 1916-18. Appointed as commander of the German Eighth Army in East Prussia in August 1914, he made his reputation for strategic insight and tactical skill at Tannenberg. In 1916 he was appointed Commander-in-Chief and was responsible (with General Ludendorff) for planning and conducting German operations until the end of the war. Served as President of Germany 1925-34 and was responsible for appointing Adolf Hitler chancellor in 1933.

Marshals Haig and Joffre

Field Marshal Paul von Hindenburg

Marshal Joseph Jacques Césaire Joffre (1852-1931), French Commander-in-Chief, 1914-16. He was a firm believer in the spirit of "the offensive" and, despite the crucial victory on the Marne in 1914, he proved incapable of seeing beyond the idea of frontal attacks, costly though they were.

David Lloyd George (1863-1945), British Prime Minister 1916-1922. Appointed Minister of Munitions in the National Ministry (May 1915) and Secretary of State for War on Kitchener's death (June 1916), he became Prime Minister on the fall of Asquith (December 1916). He did much to boost British morale and, with President Wilson of the USA and Premier Clemenceau of France, was responsible for imposing peace terms on the defeated Central Powers.

General Erich Ludendorff (1865-1937), German staff officer, served with Field Marshal von Hindenburg and considered the "brains" in a brilliant partnership of command. Appointed von Hindenburg's chief of staff in 1914, he helped to turn the tide for the Germans on the Eastern Front, where he remained until 1916. Accompanying von Hindenburg when the latter became Commander-in-Chief of the German Army, Ludendorff was responsible for much of the strategic thinking of

David Lloyd George

the later war years. Fleeing to Sweden in November 1918, he later returned to Germany and was implicated in Hitler's Beer Hall Putsch.

Tsar Nicholas II (1868-1918), the last Tsar of Russia. By 1914 he was in a weak political position, under pressure from groups intent upon change. As casualties mounted during the war years, he gradually became isolated. He was forced to abdicate in March 1917 and, along with his family, was murdered by the Bolsheviks at Ekaterinburg in July 1918.

General John Joseph Pershing (1860-1948), Commander-in-Chief of US forces in Europe in 1918, nicknamed "Black Jack." A soldier with combat experience in Cuba, the Philippines and Mexico, he led his troops to Europe on the clear

understanding that they were to act as an independent force, not under the orders of either the French or the British. In reality, however, he showed a commendable willingness to cooperate with his allies, particularly in the counteroffensive of September-October 1918.

Kaiser Wilhelm II (1859-1942), last German emperor and King of Prussia. He gloried in the militaristic traditions of the Prussian Army and did much to pave the way to war in 1914 by his policies of German aggrandizement. Once the war began, however, he lost much of his effective power to his generals and his influence declined. He abdicated in November 1918, fleeing to Holland.

Thomas Woodrow Wilson (1856-1924), 28th President of the United States. Elected on the Democrat ticket in 1912, he was a man dedicated to reform and American neutrality. As German pressure on the US increased, he was forced to lead his country into war in April 1917. In January 1918 he put forward his "Fourteen Points" for a just and lasting peace, and these became a basis for the Treaty of Versailles a year later. Unfortunately, his concentration upon foreign affairs undermined his domestic political support and he was defeated in the presidential election of 1920.

General John Joseph Pershing

Kaiser Wilhelm II

Woodrow Wilson

LAND WARFARE

When the First World War began, the fighting was expected to follow a familiar pattern. As cavalry scouted ahead, ready to attack vulnerable enemy targets, they would be supported by horse-drawn artillery. These would rush forward, unlimber and fire shrapnel shells at close range into enemy concentrations. This would prepare the way for the infantry, using rifles and bayonets.

Some experiments had been conducted, principally by the French, in concentrating field guns to achieve a greater impact. There was also plenty of evidence from past wars to suggest that such a fluid battle was unlikely, but military beliefs have a habit of dying hard.

The result was something of a shock, for although some mobile battles were fought in 1914, they soon gave way to static deadlock, dominated by the effects of the machine gun.

Firing from concealed positions, machine guns broke up infantry assaults, decimated cavalry units and forced the artillery to retire out of range. Soon, the phenomenon of the "empty battlefield" emerged, in which no soldier dared to show his face above ground level except in a prepared attack.

The use of artillery

Thereafter, the war assumed a new pattern in which armies tried to find an effective counter to the machine gun. At the artillery level, commanders explored the potential of concentrated fire – the "barrage" – delivered from behind the lines onto enemy positions about to be attacked.

Field guns such as the French 75 mm, German 77 mm and British 18-pounder – the pre-war horse-drawn guns – were dug in. They compensated for their lack of visibility by using forward observation officers, whose telephone reports of falling shot corrected errors. These guns were joined by increased numbers of howitzers, designed to lob plunging fire onto unseen targets.

Most howitzers were of 155-mm caliber, although the Germans even deployed some of 420-mm, served by a crew of 100 and capable of firing a 1,000-kg (2,200-lb) shell up to 14 km (9 miles). By calculating the weight of shot, atmospheric pressure and the effects of weather, accuracy could be improved. Also air or balloon observers corrected the targeting.

By 1916, it was not unknown for a bombardment of 2,000 guns and howitzers to go on for days before an infantry assault began. But the results were often disappointing. Enemy soldiers could escape the effects by sheltering underground.

Gun and Howitzer

Artillery was subdivided into the gun and the howitzer, each with its own characteristics and roles. The gun fired a projectile (shell) at high speed, hitting targets that could be seen. The howitzer lobbed a heavier shell, attacking targets beyond the normal vision of the gunners.

 Gun   Howitzer

A French 75-mm gun

A German 77-mm gun

A British 6-inch howitzer

Some suffered "shell shock" if the bombardment went on for long periods. The heavy weight of fire churned the ground of no man's land to a quagmire and barbed wire defenses were rarely destroyed.

The development of the tank

In such circumstances, something more was needed to break the deadlock. At a tactical level, many new weapons were tried out. Trench mortars, flamethrowers, snipers' rifles, gas shells and even attacks from the air were also used but not very successfully. What was needed was something that could cross no man's land easily.

The British pioneered the development of just such a machine, originally calling it the "landship." This was later called a "tank;" after the first examples traveled to France disguised as "water tanks."

It was a simple concept – a tracked vehicle, lozenge-shaped to cross trenches and protected by armor plate. It would open the way to infantry attacks by squashing barbed wire, overrunning machine-gun positions and forcing the enemy out of his trench defenses.

Before long, the tanks were given more offensive armament to produce

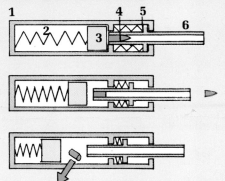

Machine gun in operation
1 Machine gun case. 2 Spring.
3 Breechblock. 4 Bullet.
5 Barrel spring. 6 Barrel.

The Machine Gun
Developed in the 1880s, it provided rapid and sustained fire. If protected by earthworks and barbed wire, it was extremely difficult to destroy. Frontal assaults were invariably suicidal.

Top: Breechblock and barrel locked together with bullet loaded.
Center: Breechblock and barrel thrown back by bullet leaving barrel.
Bottom: Breech separates and empty case is ejected.

a weapon of great battlefield potential. By 1916, the Mark I tank 7.7 m (25 ft 5 in) long, protected by 12 mm of armor and weighing 30 tons, was a formidable monster. It could crawl forward at 6 km/h (3.7 mph) and lay down fire from 6-pounders or machine guns.

In the event, the full potential of the tank was not to be realized until it had been freed from its infantry-support role. Once it appeared, backed by air power, the age of battlefield domination by the machine gun was over. Wars of movement were once more possible.

Trench-crossing Tank

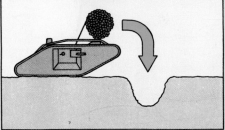

A Mark IV tank, 1917

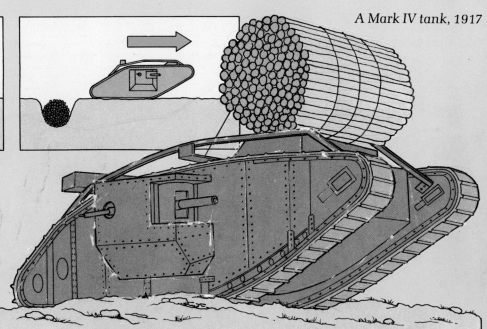

Tanks were designed to cross obstacles in no man's land. Small trenches could be negotiated using the tracks, and barbed wire could be crushed. For wider trenches special bundles of wood (fascines) were carried, to be dropped in front of the tank as a filler (see above).

TRENCH WAR

The trench system is indelibly associated with the First World War, especially on the Western Front. As soon as the battles of maneuver were over and the two sides had fought each other to a standstill in late 1914, it was only logical for the soldiers to "dig in," scraping out holes in the ground. At first these were no more than holes, supplemented by sandbags to give added protection or roofed over to create rudimentary bunkers. But as the front remained static, they gradually became more complex, until an elaborate and virtually unbreakable system emerged.

Digging deep

By the end of 1914 on the Western Front, the trenches stretched from the Swiss border to the Channel coast, and although they were not all connected in one long line, they did provide an effective barrier to attack. Facing the enemy, with barbed wire entanglements in front to prevent surprise attack, was the ordinary front-line trench, often a reworking of the original "scrape" dug out at the beginning of the deadlock.

German troops "stand-to" in a front-line trench, Western Front, 1915.

Theoretically, this should have been a carefully engineered affair, between three to four meters (10 to 12 feet) deep with sheer sides, a flat base covered with duckboards (wooden planks) and provision for shelter in dugouts or bunkers.

The soldiers responsible for defending this structure would be on constant guard against attack, placing small groups of men out in "no man's land," establishing machine-gun posts to fire on any possible avenue of approach and keeping constant watch, either by means of periscopes or by men standing on special "fire-steps" cut out of the side of the trench so that they could just see over the top. The rest of the troops would be in the trench itself, in dugouts or on sleeping shelves scraped into the trench side. As each unit would be responsible for a substantial length of front, the trenches were rarely overcrowded, except when men were preparing to mount an attack or conduct a patrol into no man's land.

Lines of communication

As the war progressed, the first line of trenches was supported by reserve lines, often extending some distance behind forward positions. In areas where the enemy artillery, mortars or snipers were particularly active, communications trenches, of equal depth to those in the first line, would connect the main positions. Reserve lines would also be deep if a

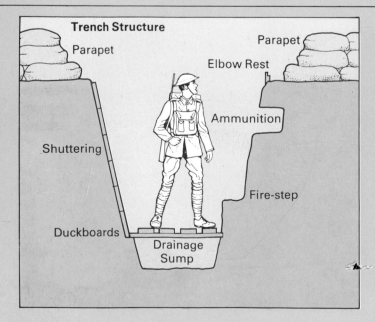

Trench Structure

Parapet

Parapet

Elbow Rest

Ammunition

Shuttering

Fire-step

Duckboards

Drainage Sump

The trench systems

The diagram on the left shows a sectional view of an "ideal" trench, complete with drainage, duckboards, fire-step and sandbag parapets. Unfortunately, few were like this in reality, suffering all the problems of disrepair as successive units used them under different conditions of battle and weather.

The plan on the right shows how the trench system evolved, with elaborate communications, support-lines, dugouts and machine-gun posts, while that far right illustrates the depth of a typical system after a few months of deadlock.

Once the system had become this sophisticated, with a second and third line of trenches behind the front line, the chances of a breakthrough by attacking forces were remote, requiring either enormous casualties or the advent of some new, devastating weapon. It was a problem that was never solved.

Standing in water for a long time caused "trench foot."

withdrawal was being prepared. Usually, however, trenches became shallower the further away one was from no man's land.

Even so, the existence of machine-gun posts, dugouts, mortar positions and firing lines in the rear, ready to be manned in the event of a threatened enemy breakthrough, was often crucial to the defense of the first line. Indeed, in February 1917 the Germans on the Western Front deliberately withdrew from their forward trenches into specially constructed bunkers and fortified positions some miles back, consolidating their defense on the so-called Hindenburg Line and presenting the Allies with a much more solid barrier to break through.

Trench duties

Life in the trenches was hard, especially in the winter or, as in 1916 and 1917, during periods of almost continuous rain. A unit would be expected to man the front line for about a week, sometimes longer, before being relieved. During that time, it was not just a case of sitting passively awaiting an enemy attack, for most commanders recognized the value of activity.

This varied according to the position of the trench along the front line, the activities of the enemy, the likelihood of an offensive and the aggressive nature of local commanders. Normally soldiers would be expected to man forward positions in no man's land, conduct patrols up to the lip of the enemy trench at night, listening for snippets of intelligence, making or breaking gaps in the barbed wire or, occasionally, mounting fighting patrols to capture enemy prisoners or just to keep the enemy alert. The opportunity for action was often welcomed, but was understandably wearing on the nerves.

A nightmare existence

For the rest of the time, the soldiers would live in the trenches, sleeping, eating and working on a shift basis. If the weather was clear, this was not always unpleasant, but if the rains came down, conditions rapidly deteriorated. Trenches would soon fill with water until men were wading waist deep. The sides of the trench would collapse and turn the soil to mud, leaving the men prone to a range of ailments and diseases. Trench foot, a particularly nasty form of cold injury, was rife, as were colds and influenza.

A poor or monotonous diet of canned food, rarely supplemented by hot meals from the rear if the enemy was active, did not help. Health and hygiene were threatened by the presence of lice and rats – the latter sometimes as big as cats from gorging on corpses. Also the perpetual threat or reality of enemy action contributed to the really atrocious conditions.

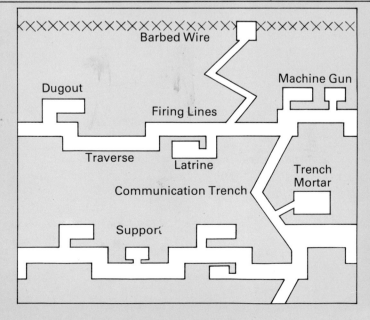

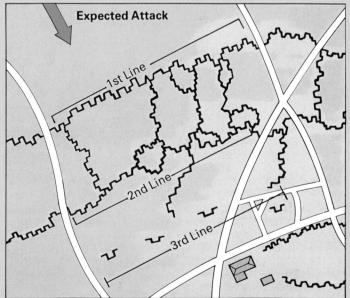

SEA WARFARE

In 1914, sea warfare was dominated by the concept of the "fleet," a powerful combination of naval vessels designed to seize control of ocean areas and maintain free passage for merchant ships carrying cargoes of vital war material. Such control could be achieved either by means of battle, in which the enemy fleet would be destroyed, or through deterrence, forcing the enemy to stay in port for fear of the losses he might suffer in battle. As the First World War progressed, it became obvious that the two main naval protagonists – Britain and Germany – preferred the more cautious approach.

Although the option of battle promised a quick result, it was safer to maintain the deterrent effect of a "fleet in being," capable of fighting but powerful enough to prevent the enemy from becoming too adventurous. In such circumstances, however, Britain enjoyed a key advantage – access to the oceans of the world – and this forced the Germans to adopt a more aggressive policy in an attempt to break out from their ports at Cuxhaven and Kiel. When this failed at Jutland in May 1916, sea warfare began to change, but the process was disguised by the continued existence of virtually intact fleets.

Battleships

The rival fleets were organized around their battleships, huge armored gun platforms that were designed to deliver a devastating attack once an engagement began. By 1914 the battleship was a formidable weapon, enjoying all the benefits of new technology. Gone were the days of close ship-to-ship engagements. New techniques of fire control, combined with dramatic improvements to the weight, accuracy and range of naval shooting, allowed the fleets to "stand off," lobbing salvos of coordinated shellfire onto a distant target.

The British had led the way, producing the *Dreadnought* in 1906, and for a short time its combination of speed, armor protection and firepower (the latter provided by ten 305-mm/12-inch guns, mounted in pairs on revolving turrets) had rendered other battleships obsolete. Some of the pre-*Dreadnought* designs remained in service, but by 1914 all the major navies of the world had adopted the new ideas and, in many cases, refined them. In the United States, the "Michigan" and "Pennsylvania" classes fitted the bill. In Germany it was the "Nassau" and "Helgoland" classes and in Britain, incorporating more secondary armament, the "Bellerophon" class. They all represented a considerable advance in technology and fighting capability.

HMS Dreadnought

The British battleship HMS *Dreadnought*, launched in 1906, was a revolutionary design. For the first time, a battleship was equipped with guns which were all of the same caliber – 305-mm (12-inch). This simplified both ammunition storage and fire control, enabling a greater weight of shot to be fired. At the same time, the 10 guns, arranged in five twin-gun turrets, gave an all-around arc of fire, and when this was married to increased speed, provided by oil-fired steam turbines, it made all previous designs obsolete. However, the lack of smaller guns was a weakness.

All-around fire power

Battle cruisers

No one expected a battleship to act on its own, for it needed not only protection against smaller vessels which might creep beneath the main armament to deliver torpedo attacks, but also "eyes and ears" to ensure that it arrived at the right place and time for battle. These duties were carried out by the other elements of the fleet.

At the top end of the scale were the battle cruisers – ships which were armed as battleships but designed to achieve greater speeds, principally by cutting down on armor plate. They were meant to scout ahead of the main fleet, searching for the enemy and, having found him, engaging his battle line while the rest of the fleet closed up. In theory, this was a reasonable idea, but the saving on armor protection was dangerous. At Jutland, the loss of three British battle cruisers showed how vulnerable they were and the concept was quietly dropped.

Light cruisers and destroyers

Of much more effect were the light cruisers, in which speed rather than firepower was stressed. They too were responsible for scouting, ranging far and wide in search of the enemy, but once he was located, their tasks were to observe, stay in visual contact and act as guides for the main fleet as it maneuvered to gain the advantages of wind (to clear gunfire smoke), sea room and surprise. Once the battle began, the light cruisers acted as protectors of the battle line, creating a screen to prevent the approach of enemy torpedo-carrying vessels.

A similar role was envisaged for the destroyers – the fastest elements of the fleet – and in both cases, the ships would be organized into "flotillas" to ensure coordination. As enemy light cruisers and destroyers were intent on carrying out exactly the same roles, separate battles would often develop at this level, while the battleships

hammered it out at a more distant range.

Changes in naval strategy

A fleet action should therefore have been a carefully choreographed affair, with lines of battleships and battle cruisers facing each other at a distance while lighter, more maneuverable vessels fought to protect them from torpedo attack. It did not always work and at Jutland a combination of poor coordination, inaccurate gunnery and a reluctance to continue the battle into a second day produced an indecisive result.

Alternative strategies were explored, particularly by the Germans. Their shift to U-boats, forcing the British to divert attention to antisubmarine warfare, with its emphasis on smaller vessels and rudimentary aircraft carriers, marked a major change in the nature of sea warfare. The days of the battlefleet, and with it the battleship, were numbered.

The working of a US twin turret 12-inch gun

1 Magazine
2 Central column
3 Projectile hoist
4 Powder hoist
5 Rammer
6 Projectile
7 Breech
8 Barrel

U-boats

U-boats usually attacked from the surface using torpedoes or, if the target could not defend itself, special deck guns, the firing of which was

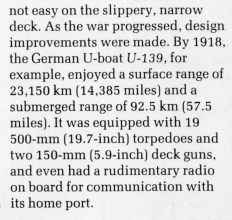

not easy on the slippery, narrow deck. As the war progressed, design improvements were made. By 1918, the German U-boat *U-139*, for example, enjoyed a surface range of 23,150 km (14,385 miles) and a submerged range of 92.5 km (57.5 miles). It was equipped with 19 500-mm (19.7-inch) torpedoes and two 150-mm (5.9-inch) deck guns, and even had a rudimentary radio on board for communication with its home port.

Periscope

Radio aerials

Deck gun

Torpedo tubes

Torpedo

AIR WARFARE

When the war began in August 1914, military aviation was in its infancy. No one had analyzed its potential beyond the obvious advantage of reconnaissance, a role which seemed to require nothing more than a good pair of eyes and an ability to fly. As a result, few specialized aircraft designs had emerged and the three main air forces – those of Germany, France and Britain – were firmly controlled by their respective armies or navies and expected to make do with whatever aircraft were available.

As these included monoplanes, biplanes, single-seaters, two-seaters, "tractors" (with the propeller at the front) and "pushers" (with the propeller at the back), it proved impossible to create a coordinated air effort, not least because of the nightmare problems of servicing and spares.

Development of the fighter

Early operations therefore were carried out by single aircraft, flying over enemy lines to observe and report troop movements. Their vulnerability to ground-fire soon led many pilots and observers to arm themselves or their planes for protection or retaliatory fire. At first, their attempts were crude – pistols, rifles, grenades and the occasional "lashed-on" machine gun. It did not take long to realize that, with such weapons, enemy aircraft could be attacked and, if not destroyed, at least forced to turn away from sensitive areas close to the front line.

The aim of the exercise was to deny the enemy the advantage of air reconnaissance while ensuring that friendly aircraft survived, so the next logical step was to produce specialized "fighter" or "scout" designs. As early as February 1915, the Royal Flying Corps (RFC) fielded the Vickers FB5 "Gunbus," a pusher design with a machine gun in the forward nacelle. Five months later No. 11 Squadron was sent to France equipped with nothing but this aircraft. It was a degree of uniformity that allowed, for the first time, a concentration of force capable of seizing air "supremacy."

Arming fighters

But a machine gun firing ahead of the pilot was clearly impossible in the more popular "tractor" aircraft without shredding the propeller blades. Also the gun itself – usually a drum-fed Lewis – proved impossible to reload with safety in mid-air. What was needed was a fixed machine gun, belt-fed from within the aircraft and positioned so that the pilot only had to fly straight at his enemy, using the direction of flight to facilitate aiming.

Before 1914, experiments had been carried out in both France and Germany using deflector plates – small metal disks set in to the blades to deflect any dangerous bullets – but these had been largely ignored.

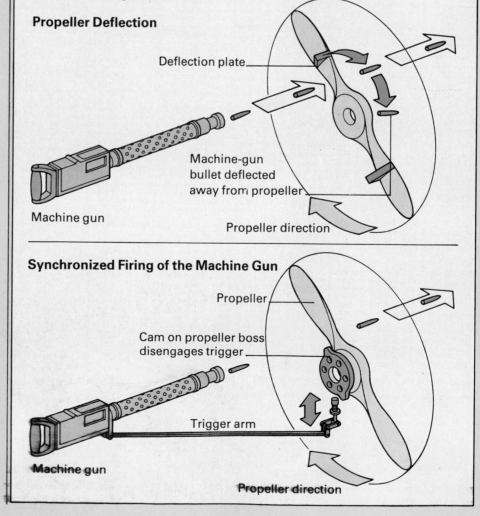

Arming the Fighter

"Tractor" aircraft, with the engine at the front, were difficult to equip with machine guns, because bullets fired straight ahead shredded the blades. Early attempts to solve this involved fitting special deflector plates to each blade. These were angled to divert bullets that might otherwise have struck them. But this was still dangerous, and it was Fokker's perfection of an interrupter gear – a cam linking the propeller to the gun which stopped the firing whenever a blade was in the way – that revolutionized the air war.

Propeller Deflection

Deflection plate

Machine-gun bullet deflected away from propeller

Machine gun

Propeller direction

Synchronized Firing of the Machine Gun

Propeller

Cam on propeller boss disengages trigger

Machine gun

Trigger arm

Propeller direction

It was left to a Dutchman, Anthony Fokker, to develop the idea of an interrupter device, designed to stop the machine gun firing whenever a propeller blade swept into view. This was first tried out on his EIII monoplane in early 1915. Unfortunately for the Allies, and despite the neutrality of the Netherlands, Fokker sold his design to the Germans.

German success

The result was the "Fokker Scourge" of 1915-16 on the Western Front, during which the British and French lost air supremacy to "aces," such as Oswald Boelcke and Max Immelmann, in their EIII "Eindekkers." It was not until an EIII had been captured intact that the Allies learned the secret of synchronized fire, and they were quick to use it in their own aircraft designs. Fighters such as the Sopwith 1½ Strutter, Sopwith Pup and Nieuport 17 helped to redress the balance, but not for long.

Dogfights

The Germans reacted with perhaps their best fighter of the First World War – the Albatros DV, armed with twin machine guns capable of firing through the propeller. They also concentrated their fighters into special *Jagdstaffeln* (squadrons) of devastating impact, ushering in the era of the "dogfight." Soon there were huge aerial encounters between dozens of aircraft trying to control the airspace over the front line, in which a new generation of "aces" prospered. Chief among these was Baron Manfred von Richthofen, nicknamed the "Red Baron" because of the color of his Albatros DV.

The Allies responded with twin-gun fighters of their own, including the Sopwith Camel, SE5 and Spad XIII, but they could not prevent disaster. The crisis came in April 1917 when the RFC, in a series of dogfights over Arras, lost almost a third of its front-line strength. By then the average life expectancy of an RFC pilot in France was less than two weeks.

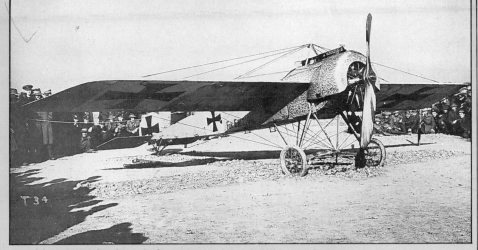

A Fokker EIII, the first fighter to use an interrupter device

Air supremacy

It took the Allies over a year to regain the initiative, for despite the development of yet more new designs, notably the superb Bristol fighter, they had to contend with German tactical innovations. One was the *Jagdgeschwader* (fighter wing or, in Allied parlance, "Flying Circus"), which involved a concentration of almost overwhelming force at selected points along the front.

In the end it was a combination of factors – German complacency, the development of the RFC "Wing" as a counter to the Flying Circus, better aircraft designs and the emergence of Allied aces such as William Bishop and "Mick" Mannock – that forced the Germans back onto the defensive in the summer of 1918. By then Americans had begun to arrive in France and by September they could field 45 squadrons, with many more in preparation. However it had been a close call. There could now be no denying that air power had added a third, potentially decisive dimension to the business of war.

The Sopwith Camel, one of the best British fighters of the war

CHRONOLOGY

1914

June 28 Assassination at Sarajevo

July 23 Austro-Hungarian ultimatum to Serbia

July 28 Austria-Hungary declares war on Serbia

August 1 Germany declares war on Russia

August 3 Germany declares war on France

August 4 Germany invades Belgium; Britain declares war on Germany and imposes naval blockade

August 6 British Empire troops enter Togoland

August 13 Austro-Hungarian troops invade Serbia

August 14-20 "Battle of the Frontiers" (Alsace-Lorraine)

August 17 Russian troops invade East Prussia

August 19-20 German defeat at Gumbinnen (East Prussia)

August 23 Germans checked at Mons (Belgium) by BEF

August 26-29 Russians defeated at Tannenberg (East Prussia)

August 26-30 Austro-Hungarians defeated at Lemberg (Galicia)

September 5-9 Germans halted at Battle of the Marne (France)

September 12-18 German withdrawal to the Aisne (France)

September 18-October 11 "Race to the Sea;" trenchline established on Western Front

October 20-November 11 British offensive, First Battle of Ypres

October 29 Turkey attacks Russia and Britain

November 1 Naval Battle of Coronel (Chile)

November 2 German naval bombardment of Norfolk coast

November 9 German raider *Emden* sunk

November 11 Russian defeat at Lodz (Poland)

November 21 British occupation of Basra (Mesopotamia)

December 8 Naval Battle of the Falklands

December 25 Unofficial Christmas Day "truce," Western Front

1915

January-April Russian offensive, Carpathians (Galicia)

January 19 First Zeppelin raid on Britain

January 24 Naval Battle of the Dogger Bank

February 1 Germany introduces bread rationing

February 4 Germany declares British waters "war zone"

February 7 German offensive, Masurian Lakes (East Prussia)

February 16-March 30 French offensive, Champagne (France)

February 19-March 18 Allied naval bombardment, Dardanelles

March 10-13 British offensive, Neuve Chapelle (France)

April 22-May 24 German offensive, Second Battle of Ypres (Belgium); first use of chlorine gas

April 25 Allied landings, Gallipoli

May 2-4 German victory, Gorlice-Tarnow (Galicia)

May 7 *Lusitania* sunk

May 9-June 18 French offensives, Artois and Champagne (France)

May 15-27 British offensives, Festubert and Aubers Ridge (Belgium)

May 24 Italy declares war on the Central Powers

June 23-July 7 Italian offensive, Isonzo sector

August 6 British landing, Suvla Bay (Gallipoli)

August 17-September 28 British advance towards Kut (Mesopotamia)

September 9-October 15 Austro-German offensive, Vilna (Russia)

September 25 Allied offensives, Champagne, Artois, Loos (Western Front)

October 5 Allied landings, Salonika

October 6-December 15 Serbia conquered by Central Powers

October 14 Bulgaria declares war on the Central Powers

November 11-22 British advance, Euphrates (Mesopotamia)

November 25-December 8 Turkish counterattack, Mesopotamia

December 6 Allied war leaders meet at Chantilly

December 8 Kut besieged by Turks

December 18 Allied evacuation of Gallipoli begins

1916

January 1-April 12 Russian offensive, Vilna

January 9 Gallipoli evacuation complete

February 21 German assault on Verdun (France)

February 25 Germans capture Fort Douaumont, Verdun

April 24-30   Easter Rising, Dublin

April 29   Kut falls to the Turks

May 15-June 19   Austro-Hungarian offensive, northern Italy

May 31   Naval Battle of Jutland

June   Arab Revolt begins

June 4-September 7   Brusilov Offensive, Eastern Front

June 9   Germans capture Fort Vaux, Verdun

July 1   British offensive, First Day of the Somme

August 27   Romania declares war on the Central Powers

August 27-September 18   Romanian offensive, Transylvania

September 15   First use of tanks, Flers-Courcelette (Somme)

November 13   British offensive on the Somme ends

November 21   Emperor Franz-Joseph of Austria-Hungary dies, replaced by Emperor Karl

December 6   Romanian capital, Bucharest, falls

December 12   British offensive, Mesopotamia

December 15   Battle of Verdun ends

1917

January 1-March 30   British advance into Palestine

February 1   Germans declare "unrestricted" U-boat campaign

February 3   US severs diplomatic relations with Germany

February 23   Germans begin withdrawal to Hindenburg Line (Western Front)

March 9   Food riots in Petrograd (Russia)

March 11   British capture Baghdad (Mesopotamia)

March 15   Tsar Nicholas of Russia abdicates

March 26-November 7   British offensives, Gaza (Palestine)

April 6   US declares war on Germany

April 8-16   Lenin travels from Switzerland to Petrograd

April 9-May 3   British offensive, Arras/Vimy Ridge (France)

April 16-May 9   French Nivelle Offensive

May 3   Mutinies in the French Army start

May 10   Britain introduces naval convoys

June 7   British attack, Messines Ridge (Belgium)

June 13   First Gotha bomber raid on London

July 31-November 12   British offensive, Third Battle of Ypres (Passchendaele)

August 21-October 24   Austro-German offensive, Galicia

October 24-31   Italian defeat, Battle of Caporetto

November 5   Rapallo Conference, Allies set up Supreme War Council

November 7   Bolshevik Revolution in Russia

November 20-30   British tank attack, Cambrai (France)

December 9   British capture Jerusalem

December 12   Armistice, Romania/Central Powers

December 15   Armistice, Russia/Central Powers

1918

January 8   President Wilson announces peace plan ("Fourteen Points")

March 3   Treaty of Brest-Litovsk (Russia/Central Powers)

March 21-April 4   German "Michael" Offensive (Western Front)

April 9-29   German offensive, Lys sector (France)

April 14   Foch appointed Allied Commander-in-Chief

April 22   British seaborne attack on Zeebrugge (Belgium)

May 19   Last Gotha bomber raid on Britain

May 27-30   German offensive, Soissons-Reims (France)

June 9-13   German offensive, Battle of the Matz (France)

June 15-24   Austro-Hungarian offensive, Piave (Italy)

July 18   Allied counterattack, Second Battle of the Marne (France)

August 8-12   Allied counterattack, Battle of Amiens (France)

August 10-13   Allied counter-attack, Bapaume (France)

September 1-30   RAF raids on German cities

September 12-16   US offensive, St Mihiel (France)

September 15-29   Allied offensive, Salonika

September 19   British victory, Battle of Megiddo (Palestine)

September 26-October 14   US offensive, Meuse-Argonne (France)

September 27-October 5   Allied offensive, Maubeuge (France) and towards Ghent (Belgium)

September 29   Armistice, Bulgaria/Allied Powers

September 30   British seize Damascus (Syria)

October 30   Italian victory, Battle of Vittorio Veneto

October 30   Armistice, Turkey/Allied Powers

November 4   Armistice, Austria-Hungary/Allied Powers

November 9   Revolution in Berlin; Kaiser Wilhelm abdicates

November 11   Armistice, Germany/Allied Powers

INDEX

Note: Numbers in bold refer to illustrations or maps

FURTHER READING

Bailey, Thomas A, and Paul B Ryan, *The Lusitania Disaster: An Episode in Modern Warfare and Diplomacy* (Free Press, 1975)

Gammage, B, *An Australian in the First World War* (Cambridge University Press, 1976)

Graves, Robert, *Good bye to All That*, rev ed (Doubleday 1956)

Horne, Alistair, *The Price of Glory: Verdun 1916* (Penguin, 1979)

Joll, James, *The Origins of the First World War* (Longman, 1984)

Lawrence, T E, *Seven Pillars of Wisdom* (Doubleday, 1966)

Liddell Hart, B H, *The Real War, 1914-1918* (Boston: Little, Brown, 1964)

Liddle, Peter, *The Sailor's War, 1914-1918* (Sterling, 1985)

Macdonald, Lyn, *They called it Passchendaele* (Topsfield, MA: Merrimack, 1984)

Marwick, Arthur, *The Deluge: British Society and the First World War* (Norton, 1970)

Remarque, Erich M, *All Quiet on the Western Front* (Little, Brown, 1929)

Ross, Gregory, *The Origins of American Intervention in the First World War* (Norton, 1972)

Seymour, Charles, *American Neutrality, 1914-1917* (Hamden, CT: Shoe String Press, 1967; orig pub 1935)

Snyder, Louis L, ed, *Historic Documents of World War I* (Westport, CT: Greenwood Press, 1977)

Tansil, Charles C, *America goes to War* (Magnolia, MA: Peter Smith, 1942)

Tuchman, Barbara W, *The Guns of August* (Macmillan, 1962)

Tuchman, Barbara W, *The Zimmermann Telegram* (Macmillan, 1966)

(NOTE: *All publishers located in New York unless specified otherwise*)

ACKNOWLEDGMENTS

Cover: Imperial War Museum; page 5: Imperial War Museum; page 7 (left): Robert Hunt Library; page 7 (right): Imperial War Museum; page 9: Bildarchiv Preussischer Kulturbesitz; page 11: Robert Hunt Library; page 14: Mansell Collection; page 16: Imperial War Museum; page 18 and inset: Popperfoto; page 19: Robert Hunt Library; page 20: Ullstein Bilderdienst; page 21 (top): Ullstein Bilderdienst; page 21 (bottom): Robert Hunt Library; pages 22-23: Popperfoto; page 24: MARS; page 25: Robert Hunt Library; page 26: Robert Hunt Library; page 27: Imperial War Museum; page 29 (top): Robert Hunt Library; page 29 (bottom): Robert Hunt Library; page 31: Imperial War Museum; page 33: Robert Hunt Library; page 36 (top): Imperial War Museum; page 36 (bottom): Imperial War Museum; page 37: Robert Hunt Library; pages 38-39: Robert Hunt Library; page 40: Robert Hunt Library; page 42: Robert Hunt Library; page 43: Central Press/Photosource; page 45: Ullstein Bilderdienst; page 46: Central Press/Photosource; page 48 (center top): Popperfoto; page 48 (center bottom): Dept of War Studies, RMA Sandhurst; page 48 (right): Popperfoto; page 49 (top): Popperfoto; page 49 (bottom left): Popperfoto; page 49 (bottom center): Dept of War Studies, RMA Sandhurst; page 49 (bottom right): Robert Hunt Library; page 52: MARS; page 53: Imperial War Museum; page 57 (top): Robert Hunt Library; page 57 (bottom): Robert Hunt Library.

PRINTED IN BELGIUM BY
proost
INTERNATIONAL BOOK PRODUCTION